A YELLOW BUTTERFLY ON AN ELEPHANT'S FOOT

A LOVE AFFAIR WITH NAMIBIA

LYDIA SCHRÖDER

Illustrated by
NICOLA FOUCHÉ

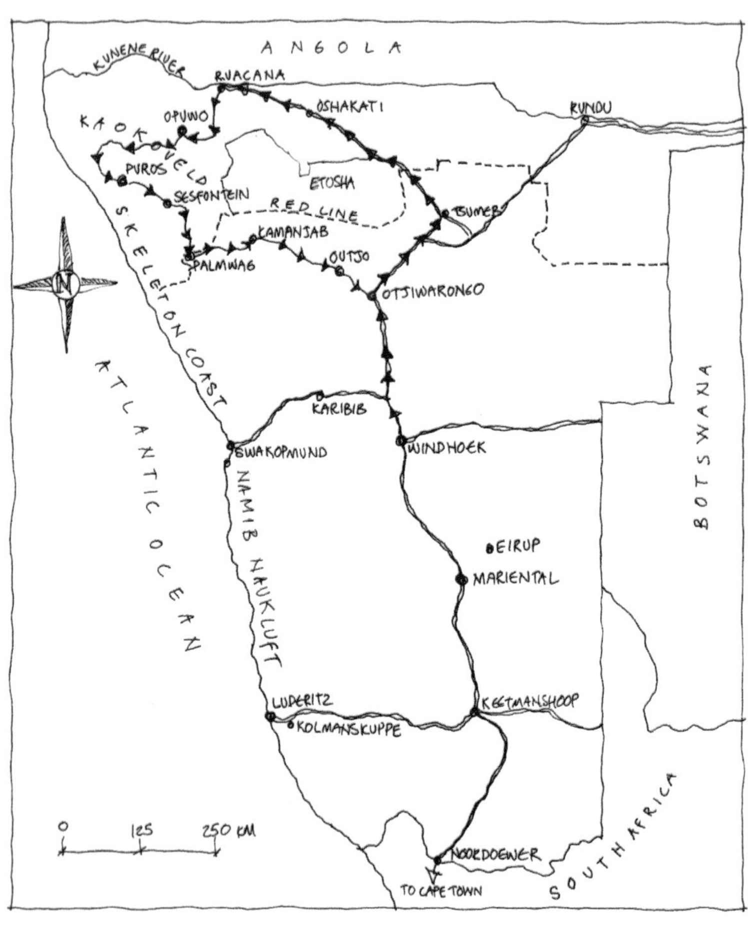
ANGOLA
KUNENE RIVER
RUACANA
OSHAKATI
RUNDU
OPUWO
KAOKOVELD
PUROS
SESFONTEIN
ETOSHA
RED LINE
TSUMEB
KAMANJAB
OUTJO
PALMWAG
OTJIWARONGO
SKELETON COAST
ATLANTIC OCEAN
KARIBIB
SWAKOPMUND
WINDHOEK
NAMIB NAUKLUFT
BOTSWANA
EIRUP
MARIENTAL
LUDERITZ
KOLMANSKUPPE
KEETMANSHOOP
0
125
250 KM
NOORDOEWER
TO CAPE TOWN
SOUTH AFRICA

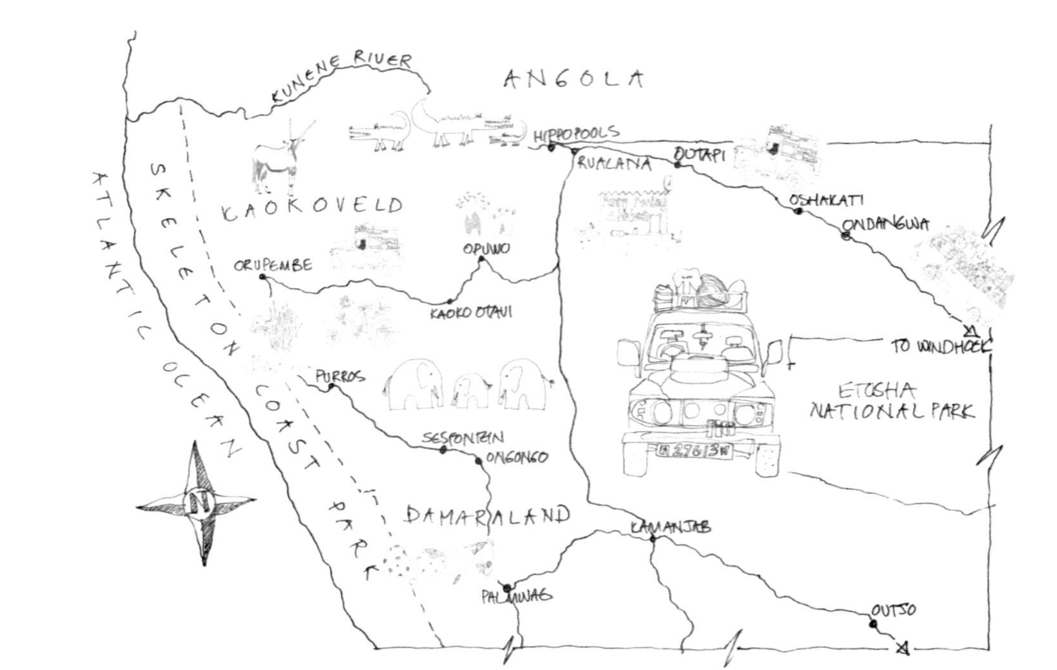
ANGOLA
KUNENE RIVER
HIPPOPOOLS
RUACANA
OUTAPI
OSHAKATI
ONDANGWA
KAOKOVELD
OPUWO
ORUPEMBE
KAOKO OTAVI
TO WINDHOEK
ETOSHA
NATIONAL PARK
PURROS
SESFONTEIN
ONGONGO
DAMARALAND
KAMANJAB
PALMWAG
OUTJO
SKELETON COAST PARK
ATLANTIC OCEAN
N

Neue Bergstraße 9,
86899 Landsberg am Lech
Germany
ISBN: 978-3-9822864-2-6 (print)
ISBN: 978-3-9822864-3-3 (E-book)

www.nicolafouche.com
nicolafouche@icloud.com

For Anthon
Nic
Alex
Louise
Luke
Dee
Nora
and everyone else populating these pages
or who helped to create this book.

CONTENTS

Chapter 1

I CAN HEAR CLEARLY NOW

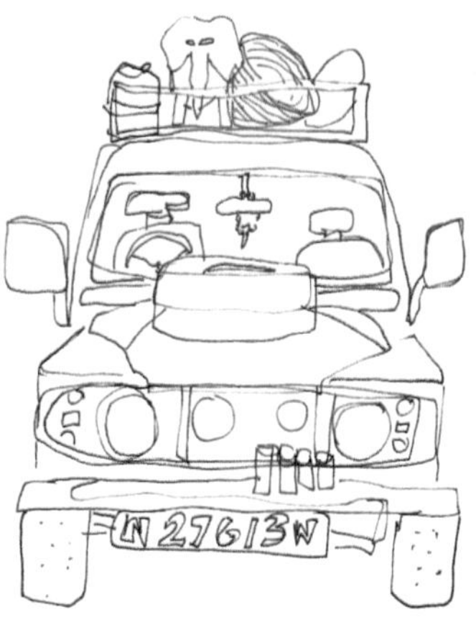

We were driving through a landscape newly washed with rain. The red clay road screamed against the green surrounding veldt. The sky pulsated with luminous blue.

A pungent aroma of wild grass, animal dung and damp soil tickled the inside of my nose.

On my previous trip to Namibia's Kunene Region, many years before, it had been late winter. The air was thick with dust and smoke. The sun disappeared into this soupy mess long before reaching the horizon, shrieking its desperation in neon orange and magenta pink. It grew larger and larger, then dissipated into the murky atmosphere, as if from sheer exhaustion; leaving us in a serene half-light.

Now it was the middle of summer, the year 2006, and we were in the midst of an outstanding rainy season.

'I can see clearly now, the rain is gone,' I spontaneously hummed the old Johnny Nash refrain.

'Did I ever tell you about the patient with the hearing problem?'

My song must have triggered a story again. Anthon has an impressive memory. I suppose one could describe it as photographic, — or does one get audio-graphic recall? — He listens to a story once and the next day he repeats it to you word for word, albeit with a little added embroidery. I maintain that his brain stores memories associatively. Say a word and he could launch into a myriad of anecdotes associated with the subject. His real-life sketches are most precious, the stories relating to his medical practice being particularly entertaining.

'Tell me,' I smiled.

He rarely needed an invitation. Shifting into a more comfortable position, he clasped Henry's steering wheel with both hands.

'Just after I'd started my surgery, I had to wear a beard to appear old enough to be someone's doctor.' He glanced in my direction to gauge my reaction.

I shook my head and smiled. I couldn't picture him with a beard.

'One morning this Important Person's Spouse, let's call her Mrs Ips, phoned the receptionist while I was in consultation with another patient. She insisted to speak to me immediately; it was a matter of Great Urgency. Assuming someone was about to die, the receptionist put the call through to me.'

He paused to search for something in the cavity next to the steering wheel and hauled a packet of cigarettes from its depths. I handed him the lighter which had migrated to my side of the Land Rover.

'"Dr Schröder," Mrs Ips said to me, her tone ever so slightly superior, "be a dear and write me a reference letter for Dr Ent; you know, the Ear Nose and Throat Specialist?" This illustrious title was articulated and emphasised just enough to allow my limited GP brain to absorb the importance of the man. "You can fax it to my husband's office. I'm sure your receptionist must have his number? It will be excellent if you can do it within the next few minutes as I'm expected at Mrs Ambassador's book club at eleven."'

He lit the cigarette, took a deep draw, then slowly blew the smoke out of the open window. He never smoked in the car with the windows shut.

I turned sideways in my seat to observe him better. The story had the makings of a performance. He loved having an audience.

'Without losing my cool and in my most professional voice, I told her to make an appointment with my front office,' he continued. 'I explained to her that I don't normally refer patients without having examined them first and that I happened to be fully booked that morning. I could hear an impatient sigh on the other end of the line.'

He pulled on the cigarette again.

'"My dear doctor," he mimicked the patient's irritation, "I do not need to be examined by a GP." She spat the word 'GP' out with derision. "I know exactly what's wrong with me. I've got a problem with my hearing." She paused again to give me time to grasp the concept. "I require the services of a specialist." I was convinced I heard her foot stamping the floor.'

'Really?' I couldn't help interrupting. 'Surely that must have revved you up a bit? If she was talking to me I would've lost it immediately.'

'How often have you seen me lose my cool when someone sets themselves up so perfectly?' His eyes twinkled.

'Not often,' I had to admit.

'Never, come to think of it,' I added after a second. 'So how did you react?'

'I decided to mimic her superior tone of voice and use the same stilted vocabulary she did,' he replied. 'So I answered: "My dear Mrs Ips, it is self-evident that you have a hearing problem". She seemed oblivious to my sarcasm. "However, the reference letter needs to contain the possible cause of your affliction, which I can only establish by doing a physical assessment. I'm at this moment sitting opposite a patient who made an appointment and will be remunerating me for my time. So if you'll excuse me."'

'And then?' I asked, a bit taken aback myself.

He released a chuckle from deep inside. 'Of course, she was shocked speechless that I wasn't intimidated by her importance. She hesitated a moment as if she didn't know what to say next, then slammed the phone down.'

'That was rather excessive,' I said.

'According to my receptionist, she called back half an hour later, requesting to book a consultation as if nothing had happened.'

He took a last draw, stretched his right arm through the open window and stamped out the end of the cigarette on the aluminium veneer covering the sides of Henry's bonnet. Then he squeezed it into an empty beer bottle wedged next to his seat for that purpose. All part of the ritual.

'And that was the end of the story?' I asked, ever impatient.

'Of course not!' he laughed. 'The next morning, as I walked into my surgery, Mrs Ips was sitting in the waiting room. Rigid, upright, hands with ringed fingers clasped over her purse. Judging by her outfit, I assumed she was on her way to have tea with another Mrs Important. She was coordinated in apricot pink from scarf to shoes. Even her lipstick seemed to match her handbag. "You look marvellous this morning, Mrs Ips," I greeted her with nonchalance. Being who I am, I couldn't help adding, "You must be on your way to another ambassadorial brunch?" She missed my hint of sarcasm and preened herself like a coquettish pigeon. "Dr Schröder," she replied, "I never leave the house if I'm not suitably attired." She looked at me with her head to the side, her eyelashes fluttering ever so slightly. I couldn't believe she was flirting with me. "But yes," she continued with a sigh and a shrug, "my social commitments are innumerable."'

We rounded a bend. An unexpected ditch appeared in the middle of the road. I swayed in my seat as Anthon navigated the Defender around its edge. The Makalani nut hanging from the rearview mirror swung in unison.

'I showed her into my examination room, inviting her to sit down,' he continued once we were on level ground again. 'I started to take down her case history. Convinced I wasn't qualified enough to diagnose her condition, she answered my questions with bored monosyllables while inspecting her apricot nail polish. Already sure of the diagnosis, I asked her to remove her earrings to allow me to inspect her ears. Like a teenager in a sulk, she took off her diamond earrings one by one and placed them in her handbag. With a you're-so-wasting-my-time look, she tilted her head to one side. I gently took hold of her earlobe and shone the otoscope inside. "Hmmm," I mumbled as if to myself. Then I ruefully clicked my tongue, shaking my head as I turned her earlobe this way and that. "Just as I suspected," I added with a grave voice. "What is it, Doctor?" she asked, suddenly concerned, "is it serious?" "Hmmm," I repeated. "Not necessarily serious, Mrs Ips, just inconvenient. How shall I explain this to you… — I paused a bit, as if I was thinking hard — …your ears are merely choc-a-block full of wax."'

Anthon started to chuckle.

'And? What then?' I urged.

'She jerked her head away from me. A bright red blush crept upwards from her neck, clashing badly with all that apricot pink. Spluttering, "This is preposterous," she leapt from the examination couch, pulled herself up to regal proportions and spat out indignantly: "My dear doctor, my personal hygiene is impeccable. How stupid of me to consult a baby faced twit of a GP younger than my own son."'

'Shame, poor you. That must've been bad for your ego?

Beard and all?' I screamed with laughter. 'So you lost a Very Important Patient that day?'

'Of course not!' he replied, his expression smug. 'Not right then, anyway. I straightened my face. In a soothing voice I said, "My dear Mrs Ips, earwax is an entirely natural substance. It has nothing to do with cleanliness. The more you push those little cotton buds into your ears, believing you're cleaning them, the deeper you compress the wax into the ear canals. I'll remove it for you in a jiffy."'

I was dumbstruck. 'Are you telling me she still allowed you to touch her ears after all this?'

'*Mein Schatz,* I may be a bit of a joker, but I still regard myself as a kind person and a good doctor. I persuaded her to sit down and proceeded to wash out her ears. I was well aware that she felt uncomfortable and a bit embarrassed and felt rather sorry for the poor woman. After I'd completed the procedure, she replaced her earrings, pushed her hair in place and smeared a fresh layer of colour over her lips. As she readied to leave, I had the brilliant idea that a harmless joke might lessen the tension and put her at ease. "Look at the bright side, Mrs Ips," I said, "when you drive home in your luxury German saloon, you can sing at the top of your voice, I can hear clearly now, the wax is gone."'

Anthon looked at me triumphantly, expecting an accolade for this piece of wit, but I was laughing too much to comply. 'How did she react?' I asked once I got my breath back.

'As I should've expected,' he answered with mock disappointment. 'She didn't get the joke. She pinched her mouth, poked her nose into the air and informed me that my services as doctor to the Family Ips would no longer be required.'

'So you did lose a patient that day,' I taunted, through peals of laughter. Yet I couldn't help being impressed with his unorthodox way of handling his patients.

'Maybe, maybe not,' he answered. 'I told her not to do me any favours. I might also have mentioned not being able to stand people without a sense of humour.'

'You certainly know how to push your luck!' I gasped. 'And then?'

'She grabbed her Gucci handbag, pirouetted on her apricot stilettos and marched out of the surgery. My receptionist and I heard her car door shut with a bang, followed by the screech of metal against metal as she grazed her Mercedes against the carport column.'

I realised I'd seen the evidence of this encounter. 'Is that the warped column next to your own parking spot?'

'The very same,' he replied.

'Surely this episode must have had consequences, apart from you losing her, the entire family, as patients?'

'It had wonderful consequences,' he laughed. 'Three weeks later she arrived at the surgery with a rather embarrassed smile and a bottle of Cognac, apologising profusely.'

I looked at him in disbelief. 'What happened?'

'I never found out, but I've got a good idea. Want to hear what I think? She must've told her husband the story, hoping he'd be so angry at me that he'd come and bash my head in or something. Instead, he thought it was hilarious and just about rolled on the floor laughing. She banished him to sleep on the couch for at least a week.' He cracked one of his deep booming laughs, then continued: 'The other possibility is that she told the story to her book club. To her disappointment, the other ladies took my side. Most of them, including Mrs Ambassador, were patients of mine.

Ultimately she must've admitted I solved her problem with the minimum of discomfort to herself and her important schedule. But I was impressed that she did come to apologise, though. It must've taken some guts. Her husband's final punishment? She probably pinched one of his own bottles of Cognac to give to me.'

I looked at the man sitting next to me. Handsome, with a bandana tied around his head, he seemed more like a soft-hearted, idiosyncratic youngster than a medical doctor in his mid-forties. He fitted as perfectly into the old Defender as it in turn fitted into the rugged Mopane veldt we were driving through. Yet, in Windhoek, he was known as the doctor with the bow ties and the unconventional surgery, filled with paintings, antique furniture, oriental rugs and classical music.

'A Land Rover driver always sits with his Landie under his arm,' was his quirky description of the way the driver's elbow as a matter of course hangs over the opened window sill, 'and my window needs to be open all the time, as the air conditioning system seldom works for longer than the first eight hours after being repaired.'

He felt my gaze and turned to look at me.

'So why do you still drive this old Land Rover?' I asked.

I've never been an automobile person. I recognise them by their colours and little else. Don't try to impress me with the car you own, it's mostly lost on me. My brain sorts vehicles according to hue and general shape: boxy, rounded, slick, big cars, small cars, SUV's. Closer to the logo I've got a chance to act as if I were knowledgeable, with an 'aha, what a smart Merc!' Or BMW, Toyota, or Audi, for that matter.

Anthon introduced me to the Land Rover versus Toyota feud. His facetious theory deals with Land Rover People and

Toyota People. Before leaving for the Kaokoveld, a Land Rover Person will carefully pack crystal glasses and a couple of bottles of vintage red into his Landie. The Toyota driver buys the largest Engel he can find and fills it with beer, brandy and coke. And maybe a box of wine. *Dooswyn*, as we call it in Afrikaans, the cheap plonk sold in a five-litre foil bag fitted with a plastic tap and packaged in a cardboard box. Prejudiced, I must agree, but since he'd shared the joke with me, I've been secretly amazed at how often it's got a ring of truth to it. A bit like the Apple versus Microsoft debate amongst architects.

'Henry's fifteen years old,' he replied. 'He's done nearly three hundred thousand kilometres and has never let me down. We may not be able to keep up with a Toyota on a tarred road, but when we get into the bush, he chugs along; uphill, downhill, through dongas and over rocks. If anything does go wrong, which rarely happens, the problem can mostly be fixed with a piece of wire or a plastic tie down. That's all I need to reach a service station. Even mechanics in the remotest villages can work on an old Defender engine.'

'You've persuaded me,' I said. I'll take reliability over speed any day.

'Do you know what Land Rover's official slogan is?' he looked at me, mischief written all over his face.

I knew I was putting my foot in it again but felt obliged to say something. 'The best four by four by far?'

'Correct,' he said.

'And Toyota's?' he asked again.

Expecting a catch, I gave this one a skip, settling for replying with a blank stare instead.

'The best four by four on tar!' He exploded with his habitual booming guffaw.

'Men and their toys,' I chuckled.

We settled back into silence.

Taking his left hand in mine, I allowed the rhythm of the fence poles guarding the sides of the road to lull me into a trance. My thoughts drifted wherever they wanted to go.

I arrived in Namibia in the late nineties, with a husband, two small daughters and a crumbling marriage. Since my first excursions into the Namib, I'd been mesmerised by the immense spaces and grandeur of the country. A few years and a long story later, I met this man; this soft soul hiding beneath his jovial jester exterior. We crisscrossed the country together. Before, I had experienced her landscapes from roads passable by a two by four vehicle, either tarred or good quality gravel. He opened her heart to me, her inaccessible secret valleys, her vast plains expanding into infinity, her unending desert tracks; he and Henry, his faithful old Land Rover Defender.

Henry is rigged out to provide those comforts indispensable when undertaking a journey through the Namibian wilderness. He boasts a rooftop tent, which not only folds open in a matter of minutes but also provides a safe and comfortable place to sleep. He's fitted with an extra battery for the Engel, that quintessential camping fridge without which no true Namibian will attempt a 'safari,' as the European tourists love to call it. He also has an extended diesel tank allowing us to cover long distances without counting the kilometres to the next filling station. Which might or might not have diesel. Henry even has a kitchen in the form of two drawers containing all the essentials to prepare a magic meal in the remotest of places: a corkscrew, two glasses, a few bottles of wine, a small bottle of olive oil, balsamic vinegar, a salt and pepper grinder; not to forget the two-cup percolator and a tin of ground coffee. The best feature, however, is the built-in water tank, complete with tap, hidden next to the exhaust. For me, luxury consists of a cup of water for brushing my teeth and two cups more, warmed over the fire, for my 'bath' before we go to bed. Henry provides this as well.

The vehicle bounced over a hollow in the road, jerking me back to the present.

'Can you reach the Stanley?' Anthon read my mind. 'A cup of coffee will go down well right now.'

I reached behind my seat to get hold of the flask where it was wedged to prevent it from falling onto its side; although a Stanley flask is so well designed it seldom leaks, even if you stand it on its head. I poured us a communal mug of coffee.

'Why is this Defender called Henry?' I asked. I've been meaning to get the answer to this question for some time. 'I thought all British cars are supposed to be female.'

'Good question,' Anthon replied. 'I bought him from good friends of mine, who lived in Windhoek for a couple of years; an Englishman and his headstrong Scottish wife. She named him Henry. I believe giving an automobile a male personality was one of her Scottish acts of defiance against the English. I took him over from them when they were transferred back to Europe, but the name stuck.'

I savoured my share of the coffee, taking care to wait for a smooth stretch of road before I brought the cup to my lips, then handed it to Anthon.

'You asked me earlier why I still drive this old Landie,' he reflected. 'For me, driving on a gravel road with Henry is a type of stress release therapy. When I felt overworked, I loaded my boys into Henry and took them camping at Bloedkoppie. When I noticed that any of my good friends were severely stressed, I lured them into taking a break by suggesting a camping trip to Spitzkoppe or a fishing trip to Terrace Bay. They hardly ever declined. You know the old question of what you'll grab when your house is on fire?' he asked with mock gravity.

'Henry? I suppose?' I had to assume the obvious.

'Of course! And that's exactly what I did when I packed up my previous life. Except that I loaded my Jura coffee machine on the front seat first.' Once again Anthon burst into good humour. Little could keep him down for long.

Chapter 2

LET'S TAKE THE SCENIC ROUTE

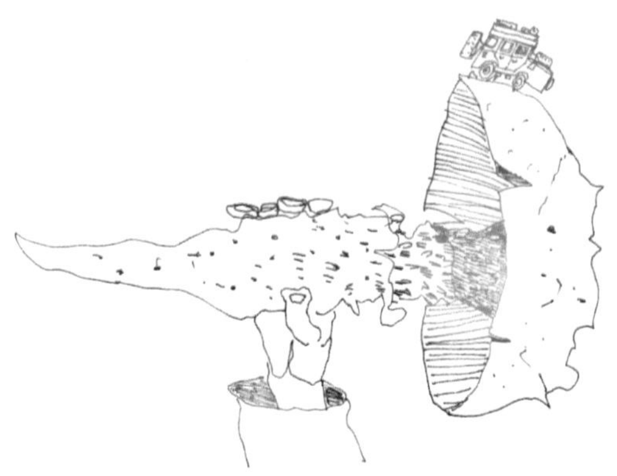

The monotony of the green Mopane veldt and the endless gravel road dragged me back into the whirlpool of thoughts stirred up by the hum of the Defender's engine.

Working as a professional in Namibia is a challenge, even if you only practise in the capital city, Windhoek. I call

Windhoek a 'city' with apprehension. The total number of inhabitants is no more than 230,000 souls; in Europe a town, in China a village. In defence of the title, Namibia's entire population is estimated to consist of about 2,5 million people, depending on who's counting. They rattle around in a country of close to 850,000 square kilometres. As Anthon likes to explain to his friends and relatives fresh from Germany: In most parts of Namibia there are square kilometres per person, not people per square kilometre.

I glanced at him furtively. His concentration focused beyond the horizon, driving his vehicle was an extension of self.

'You enjoy being a rural doctor at times, don't you?' I noticed how my question brought him out of his trance. His entire posture relaxed.

'I love it,' he replied.

'Any particular reason?' I prodded.

'I enjoy helping people, making their lives better,' he answered. 'So many rural Namibians suffer from conditions which are simple and inexpensive to treat, should they be able to get the correct diagnosis and medication. Once in a while, I need a break from 'lifestyle' diseases. Especially after having listened to more than one teenager complaining about depression in a week. Most have affluent parents, a monthly allowance equal to the minimum national wage, television and laptop of their own and attend the best private schools. Yet they're convinced they've got nothing to live for.'

That brings me to why we were bouncing along a gravel road in Henry. Having left Windhoek two days earlier, we were now on our way to Opuwo. From there we intended to explore the isolated expanse to Orupembe. On our map, the distance between the two dots had been indicated as 125km. Unbeknown to us, this would take us five hours to drive. In Namibia, a line on a map tells you little about the road and a dot next to a name seldom guarantees the existence of any modern amenities.

At the time of this journey, in addition to his GP practice in Windhoek, Anthon acted as the company doctor for Namibia's national electricity provider. Once a month he had to perform staff medicals at their hydroelectric power plant in Ruacana, close to our northern border with Angola. Not far from there, the mighty Kunene River crashes into a gorge with enough force to supply two-thirds of the electricity needed by the entire country.

I was the sole partner and only employee in my own architectural practice in Windhoek. As most of my work was done on a laptop anyway, I loved to accompany him on these trips. Ruacana was located nine hundred kilometres north-west of Windhoek. We preferred to take the direct road there and the scenic route home. Why not make a detour by way of Opuwo and from there further west into the desert? Perhaps spend a night on the edge of the Skeleton Coast to cleanse our souls and allow our spirits to soar. From there we might drive back through the vastness of the Kaokoveld and Damaraland, find another place to sleep along the way and with luck come across a desert elephant or a herd of Hartman's zebra. We've got the opportunity to combine work and leisure. International tourists pay a fortune for the privilege. For us, it costs a tank of diesel, an oryx fillet and a bottle of wine. And our time.

In 2006 most rural roads in Namibia were still constructed of good quality gravel.

We used to joke that there was a single tarred road

running lengthwise all the way from South Africa, through Namibia and into Angola and two more across the country, connecting Botswana and Johannesburg to the Atlantic Ocean. For the rest, you had to be satisfied with unpaved roads, ranging from excellent graded carriageways to rugged two wheel tracks.

On this occasion, we drove directly to Ruacana along the main tarred route from Windhoek, called the B1. Not my favourite journey, due to the number of animals and taxis encountered after crossing the Red Line at Oshivello. The Red Line? The colloquial name was given to the east-west veterinary fence stretching continuously across Botswana and Namibia to the edge of the Skeleton Coast Park. Its purpose was to prevent the spread of Foot and Mouth Disease to the uninfected southern regions.

Before Independence, the northern regions of Namibia used to be known as Wamboland as it belonged to the Owambo tribes. After Independence, it was divided into four regions, Omusati, Oshana, Ohangwena and Oshikoto. As they all start with an 'O' everybody refers to them as the 'O' regions. But the name Wamboland is still widely used to describe the portion of these regions located north of the Red Line

From Windhoek to Oshivello the B1 is fenced off from the adjacent farms, keeping domesticated animals off the road. To the north of Oshivello, the land is farmed communally. Here fences are rarely encountered.

The rural farmers love to own donkeys, although up to now no-one could really explain to me why. They seem to be of little use. They're neither slaughtered for their meat nor widely used for transport. They compete with cattle for scarce grass and water. Yet they are everywhere. For some obscure reason, they love to loiter on tar rather than in the safety of the dusty countryside. As one might already suspect, this habit of theirs often causes sensational vehicle accidents.

Donkeys aren't the only animals allowed to roam freely in Wamboland; cattle, goats and chickens also have free range. And in this part of the world 'free range' isn't a fashionable term related to the possible nutritional value of the livestock. As a result, most heavy transport vehicles delivering goods to Oshakati and Angola are fitted with massive bull bars. These are designed to lessen a possible impact and protect the driver from certain death should a collision with a large animal be unavoidable.

According to Anthon, on one of his previous trips, he saw the strangest spectacle approaching in the distance: It appeared to be a donkey with four legs on the ground and four legs sticking up into the air. As he came closer, he realised what he was seeing was a live donkey carrying a dead donkey, strapped legs-into-the-air to its back. The owner of the dead donkey must've decided the only way to retrieve the body of his animal was to transport it on the back of its unfortunate donkey relative.

To make the driving experience even more interesting, most of the region's inhabitants use taxis as their main form of transport. In our country, as in many other parts of the world, taxi drivers have their own set of traffic rules. Anthon is of the opinion they've got the right of way, the left of way and any other way they please.

North of the Red Line their driving habits are even more fascinating. Regardless of the speed limit announced next to the road, taxis either crawl or drive like lunatics.

Headlights are a fashion accessory and hardly ever used

after dark. The firm belief that switching on your lights will adversely affect your fuel consumption is widely held.

You're the driver of a taxi and need to turn right in the next two hundred meters? No problem. Move over to the right hand, oncoming lane, as soon as that lane becomes clear of approaching vehicles. This will allow the cars behind you to continue in the left lane without having to slow down when you eventually reach your turnoff. It's called good manners.

What to do when a car unexpectedly approaches from the front, in its rightful lane? Easy, you even have two options. You can go for the difficult solution and push your way back into the left lane, perhaps adding a scratch to your own vehicle and really upsetting the drivers in front of and behind you; or you can simply move onto the gravel to the right-hand side of the road and continue there until you reach your turnoff.

This brings the opposite situation to mind, where you might want to turn into the busy road from a side street. This is really straightforward, or *einfach*, as a true Namibian would say: drive next to the road, either side might do, until there's an opening in the traffic. Then cross over to the correct lane.

So, dear reader, having left Windhoek around mid-morning, one reaches this wondrous world, where right is left and light is reft, —more about that later—, during late afternoon, when the driver and his passenger might both be fairly tired. As the day fades, this already nervous passenger is confronted with oncoming cars to the left and the right, cars sometimes going in the same direction as ours, but on the wrong side of the road and stationary donkeys in the middle of the road. People, cattle, goats and chickens cross wherever they please and few vehicles drive with their headlights switched on.

No wonder we prefer taking the scenic route back.

The tiny hamlet of Ruacana is situated on an escarpment high above the Kunene River. We usually stayed at the lodge in the village, as it was situated right next to the clinic where Anthon had to conduct his medical examinations. Most of the town's inhabitants were employed, or related to someone who was employed, by the Namibian electricity provider. It followed that everybody knew the doctor.

On this particular trip, we arrived in Ruacana as dusk was falling.

'I'm going to make a quick stop at the filling station,' Anthon said. 'We might as well fill Henry now. And my cigarettes are low.'

As we pulled into the service station, Jeannie, the shop owner, came running over to the car.

'Doc Anthon!' she panted, drops of perspiration beading on her forehead, 'Doc Anthon, the falls are running. You've never seen it this full. It's more spectacular than Vic Falls!'

Realising she'd completely forgotten to greet us first, she added a bashful 'Sorry Doc, good evening Doc, good evening Mrs F.'

Anthon could barely suppress his excitement. Jumping out of the still idling Henry he gave Jeannie a hug. 'This is wonderful news!' he exclaimed.

Jeannie wiped the perspiration off her face. Running around in Ruacana was a stifling matter, especially at this time of year.

Anthon rushed to my side of the vehicle where I was still struggling to straighten my cramped legs. Without warning, he lifted me off my seat. 'We're camping at Hippo Pools tomorrow night,' he shouted, attempting to swing me through the air. I clung to him best I could, praying he wouldn't trip over the isle where the pumps were mounted.

By now Jeannie was positively glowing with satisfaction.

While the filling station attendant was filling Henry's tank, Anthon asked Jeannie, 'Could you perhaps organise us some ice and a round of *boerewors* for tomorrow?'

'But of course, Doc Anthon,' she beamed, thrilled to have been the first to tell the doctor the good news. 'I'll even prepare you some *braaibroodjies,*' she added eagerly.

'You're a star, Jeannie,' he replied. 'We'll pick up everything at around lunchtime, as soon as I've finished at the clinic. We planned on eating at the lodge this evening and tomorrow night, so we didn't pack enough food for the extra meal, but this calls for a celebration.'

'Oh, and we'll need some butter,' he added. Then, as an afterthought, 'Jeannie, would you mind lending us a pan as well? It's the one thing I didn't think of packing. I'll return it to you when we pass through Ruacana on our way back from Hippo Pools.'

'Sure Doc,' she answered.

'Why do we need the pan?' I was a bit perplexed by the last request.

'Tomorrow evening you'll eat your first Omajowa, *alfresco,* next to a magnificent river. For that, we need a pan. And best of all, chances are great we'll have the entire place to ourselves.' He was extremely satisfied with how the trip was panning out.

'Of course!' I remembered. 'We've got those huge mushrooms you bought by the side of the road earlier. You'll have to bum a pinch of nutmeg as well.'

Anthon went into the shop to buy his cigarettes and pay

for the diesel. I got back into Henry and mulled over the day's trip.

Twelve hours before, I was oblivious to the existence of something called an Omajowa. About halfway between Okahandja and Otjiwarongo, Anthon suddenly braked hard, then reversed to where a man was standing next to the road holding something looking like a little fat umbrella.

'Have you ever eaten Omajowa, *Mein Schatz*?' he asked. I was still recovering from the shock of the sudden change in Henry's direction of travel.

'A what?' I must've looked fairly dumbfounded since he started laughing.

'An O-ma-yo-va. Come along and bring your camera.' He scratched around behind his seat. His hand appeared clutching two cotton shopping bags. We walked to where the man was standing, holding the most astonishing mushroom I've ever seen. The head wasn't fully opened, but already at least thirty centimetres in diameter; the size of a dinner plate. Its stem was more than half a metre long and so thick his hand could hardly close around it. At the bottom, its root tapered to a sharp point. On top of its dome, a veneer of cracked, coffee-coloured crust overlaid the smooth white skin underneath. Fragments of red earth still clung to it, proclaiming its journey upwards through the soil. The fins underneath the head were delicate, like porcelain, in sharp contrast to the robustness of the apex and the stalk. It was phenomenal.

After the customary lengthy Oshiwambo greeting, Anthon asked the man if I could take a few photographs while they negotiated a price for the mushrooms. We left with two lovely specimens of which the domes were still half closed. Wrapped in the bags, he made space for them in Henry's drawer. Here it was always fairly cool.

'Why did you choose the smaller ones?' I asked.

'They should open during the day. You'll see how much larger they'll be by tonight. It's better than taking a fully opened mushroom which might already be infested with bugs. You must realise, they're a delicacy for all local living creatures. Apart from people, kudus, gemsbok and an entire array of insects love them.'

'How on earth are we going to cook them? Or does one eat them raw, like that?'

'We'll get someone at the lodge to cook them for us, on my instruction. I hope they've got nutmeg. Like all special foods, it's best to keep it simple. I prefer to clean it and fry the slices in butter, with a little salt and nutmeg. Omajowa is food for the Gods. I can't believe you've never eaten it.'

'I've never seen it in a shop,' I said. 'Come to think of it, I've never even heard of an Omajowa. Where does one get hold of it?'

'Of course one must know about it to look out for it. And no, you can't buy it in a shop,' Anthon explained. 'You need friends on a farm or a reason to be on the road just about now. You only get them this time of year and only if it's rained at the right time at the right place. They grow on termite hills after the first rainstorms of the season. The interesting thing is, this only occurs on some anthills, not on all of them.'

'Why would that be?'

'Nobody really knows. One of my patients, who's a naturalist, explained to me that the termites cultivate miniature fungus gardens deep down in their colony. They tend it with chewed up grass and leaves and in return, the fungus spores change the organic material into simple sugars which are more easily digested by the termites. With the first heavy downpour, the soil is still dry and cracked, which allows water to seep down into the garden. This activates the fungus to shoot out a few giant stalks, which push up through the soil to the base of the mound, eventually appearing above ground as these wonderful Omajowas we just bought.'

By the time we had reached Ruacana, I'd forgotten all about the mushrooms in Henry's drawer. Now all the talk of food made my stomach rumble.

'How far to the lodge?' I asked.

'Just around the corner, *Mein Schatz*. Don't worry, we'll be in time for dinner!' he read my mind.

As we left the service station, he started chuckling to himself. 'Just about a year ago Jeannie also came running out to tell me a story. Did I ever tell you about it?'

'Refresh my memory?' So much had happened since the previous year, my memory bank was starting to resemble a paella of experiences. I had to grab the tip of a tentacle to see what would come out.

'She came up to my door, looking concerned. "Doc," she whispered, first checking no one else was listening. "There was a man here this morning. He asked all sorts of questions about you. How often you come up here, what you do when you're here, whether you bring any women along. I told him that you always come alone and all you do is work, work, work. Doc, are you in trouble?" "Does he drive a red car?" I asked. "Yes Doc, he does! So d'you know him?" I just sighed and told her I was getting divorced and suspected that the other party must've employed a PI to spy on me; that I'd often seen this car parked across from my apartment in

Windhoek. "What?" Jeannie was shocked. "You're being spied on?" Then she got this smug look on her face. "Leave it to us, Doc, we'll sort him out! Nobody's going to mess with our Doc Anthon!"'

This time I was the one who burst out laughing. Yes, I now remembered the story. It took an interesting twist, but that should best be told another time, in another book.

Chapter 3

THE SOURCE OF THE STONE

Hippo Pools is a community campsite situated on the Kunene, a short distance from the foot of the Ruacana Falls. Although named after the town, the waterfall is located about twenty kilometres from Ruacana itself and reached by descending along a mountain pass to the bottom of the valley.

As southern Angola was experiencing an abundant rainy season, masses of water gushed over the sheer cliff forming the waterfall. The informed traveller to Namibia might know seeing this spectacle in its full majesty is a rare treat. Most of the year it's bone dry and a disappointing non-event. Especially if you drove miles out of your way to see a waterfall and end up looking at a bare dry rock face instead. The reason? The Kunene River originates in the Angolan Highlands. From here it flows south before it takes a wide swerve to the west until it touches the man-made part of the border between Namibia and Angola. —This straight line was literally drawn on a map by the German and Portuguese overlords to demarcate the division of their colonial spoils. And also to cut the troublesome Oshiwambo tribes in half, thereby diminishing their power. Drawn with a ruler, it starts from the exact position where the Kunene River disappears over the edge of the escarpment and the river takes over as the border between the two countries.— The water which used to crash into this gorge is now retained in the Calueque Dam, built further north in Angola, while a portion of it was diverted through a manmade tunnel to drive the turbines of the Ruacana hydroelectric plant. Which in turn allows Namibians to switch on their lights and watch television. It's only when the river is in full flood that the superfluous water creates one of the most remarkable natural wonders in northern Namibia.

Armed with a spray can of mosquito repellant, a similar can sporting huge red letters professing Death to All Flying Insects, two citronella candles and Jeannie's neatly packed dinner ingredients, we left the village around mid-afternoon. Huge rainclouds towered in the distance. The air was hot and sticky, glueing our clothing to our bodies.

Driving down to the Kunene is always an impressive experience. A good tarred road had been built to service the hydroelectric plant. This provides for a pleasurable descent. The escarpment drops sharply, opening breathtaking vistas over the Angolan highlands where the Calueque Dam shimmered like a slither of silver in the distance. Fleshy stemmed African Star Chestnut Trees anchored between various sizes of ochre boulders, strewn about as if left behind after a game of marbles played by the local giant's children.

'This is where Pete brought me when we were sourcing stone for one of my favourite projects.' I recognised the hill we were passing.

'What do you mean, you had to 'source stone' for the project?' Anthon asked.

'A long story, how much time have you got?' I joked.

'About twenty minutes to the Falls,' he looked at his watch. 'I'll drive slowly. Fire away!'

'Well,' I began, 'haven't I told you anything about it yet?'

'Nope. So I guess you'd better tell me now?' His eyes twinkled.

'It was one of the most interesting buildings I had designed, up to that point anyway. The brief was for a new reserve bank facility to service northern Namibia. My boss instructed me to run with it. This meant I was able to design the building, prepare most of the documentation drawings, coordinate the design with the other consultants, take it to site and see it through right until completion. Most of the other firms I had worked for loved to shunt me from design to design. They reckoned I was more valuable as producer of pretty pictures.'

'Wasn't it a huge job for one architect to handle?' Anthon asked.

'It was. And technically intricate, especially the security part. Our office was short of staff. All the other architects were as overloaded as I was. I had two technicians to help me. Without Vera and Heide I would've had a nervous breakdown, I suppose. I loved every moment, though. We worked non-stop to complete it on time. We designed every junction, chose every single fitting, all materials, you name it. When the building was finally completed and handed over to the client, I fell into a depression. It was like the end of a love affair.'

'Where did the stone come in?' he drew me back to my original story.

'You're right. I'm supposed to tell you about the stone. But I'll have to explain a bit of my design philosophy for you to understand the stone part.'

'I'm ready,' Anthon ragged me. 'Come test the medical man's understanding of things esoteric.'

I shot him a suspicious look but decided to bare my architectural soul anyway.

'One faces many challenges when designing public buildings in a more rural African context, such as Oshakati,' I began. 'One of the most difficult is marrying the first world, often rather glitzy, aspirations of the new bureaucracy with a more authentic sense of place. The committee you work with is seldom interested in concepts such as relevance to the environment and climate, let alone the realities hampering an underdeveloped region.'

'Such as?' he asked.

'Most construction materials and equipment had to be trucked to Oshakati, to Namibia, for that matter. We do not produce glass, aluminium, ceramic floor tiles, you name it. Subcontractors, all specialist workers, have to come from elsewhere and find a place to stay. And then you have a client who visualises Dubai but has a rural African government budget available. And who cannot understand why we, as architects, are bothered about the environmental and social impact of what we design.'

I paused to take a deep breath after such a mouthful. How does one explain, to someone outside one's profession, the difficulty of persuading a client that a building may be 'his', in that he or the organisation he stands for is providing the money for it, but that its impact is on the greater society and environment; the people working in it, the community relating to the spaces around it?

'It's okay, *Mein Schatz,*' he smiled. 'I understand. I deal with the First-World-Wants versus Third-World-Resources reality all the time. So how did you resolve all the contradictions? Is this what you needed the stone for?'

'Yes. We decided to contrast modern materials like aluminium and glass, with natural stone, preferably sourced locally,' I explained. 'Only problem was, there isn't a single rock to be found in Wamboland. Only fine white *oshana* sand. To find natural stone one had to collect it here, in the Ruacana area, and transport it the 180km back to Oshakati by truck.'

Anthon laughed, 'you're absolutely right. The entire area is devoid of rock.'

'Pete was one of the subcontractors on the project, appointed to do the stonework,' I continued. 'He was well acquainted with this area. He suggested to Gunther, the contracts manager, that we make a trip up here to the Kunene River to see if we couldn't find suitable local rock. They were amazing guys to work with. Both in their early fifties at the time, they had much more construction experience than I had. Yet they had high regard for my knowledge as a fellow professional and always treated me with the greatest respect. You've met Pete. He's a massive Afrikaner man. More than six feet tall and as strong as he was huge.'

'I have,' Anthon recalled. 'He's that colossal guy with the black hair and beard with whom we had coffee in Oshakati last year?'

'That's him,' I answered. 'He filled the front seat of his Ford double cab *bakkie* completely. Gunther, a German Namibian, wasn't quite as large, but still a solid piece of a man. We drove up here from Oshakati and spent the night at the same lodge where you and I normally stay. Ever the gentleman, Gunther wanted me to sit in front with Pete. I told him not to be silly, I was by far the smallest and had the shortest legs. It would've been ridiculous for him to squash into the cramped back seat of Pete's double cab.'

Anthon looked at me with a grin. 'Just imagine, we could've been here at the same time, unbeknown to each other.' Then he shook his head. 'Nah. I would've remembered your face.'

I ignored the interruption. 'Anyway, that evening there was a mighty thunderstorm while we were having dinner on the lodge's verandah. The experience was dazzling. For twenty minutes the rain came down as if the bottom had dropped out of an old rusted zinc bucket. Each flash of lightning was accompanied by an ominous electrical crackle; completely in sync, like the clap of a massive whip, followed by a moment of suspense. Until the heart-stopping crash rolled over the valley, ricochetting back to us from the opposite side of the river. I was terrified out of my mind.'

'I can just imagine,' Anthon laughed, quite unsympathetic. 'I know how our Namibian thunderstorms spook you.'

'Once the storm was over, we felt a serious drink was in order. Pete wanted to know whether I've ever been in a *shebeen*. Of course I hadn't been. Where would I have had the chance to go for drinks in one of the local Oshiwambo pubs? Anyway, there was a shebeen down the road from the lodge...'

'It's still there. It's called Fanny Resting Shebeen.' Anthon laughed.

'...and we decided to walk there.' I joined Anthon's laughter, remembering the name of the place. 'From the outside, it appeared to be a tiny brick block with a tin roof, but inside it was quite charming. A long wooden counter divided the space in two while a bare electric bulb cast a soft yellow glow over the bar. Pete and Gunther ordered beer and were promptly presented with a quart bottle each. "What the Meme wants to *dlink*?" the Oshiwambo bartender asked me. I had no idea what he meant.'

Anthon gave a chuckle.

'Pete noticed my confusion. "He wants to know what you want to drink," he whispered. Afterwards they explained the entire 'R' and 'L' thing to me, how many of the northern Namibians switch the two sounds when they speak English or Afrikaans.'

'One gets used to it,' Anthon confirmed.

'Back to the shebeen, as beer isn't my thing, I thought to keep it simple and ask for a gin and tonic. Scratching under the counter, the barman came up with an entire half litre bottle of gin and a litre of tonic, both still sealed and lukewarm. These he placed in front of me with a flourish. Seeing my consternation, Gunther asked him for a glass. And could he perhaps also bring some ice and lemon? With a big smile he disappeared through the back door, reappearing five minutes later with a zinc bucket full of ice and a huge lemon. Pete and Gunther went into fits of laughter. Apparently, my mouth was hanging open. I should've realised I wouldn't be served a single tot in a glass when they were served quart bottles of beer. Somehow I didn't make the deduction that you could only buy in bulk at this shebeen.'

Anthon crackled with laughter. 'Did you eventually manage to assemble your gin and tonic?'

'Of course,' I answered. 'How could I disappoint the bartender? Pete took out his pocket knife to slice the lemon and there was more than enough ice to cool both the bottle of gin and the litre of tonic. The remainder we left on the counter as part of the barman's tip.'

'And the rocks?' he nudged me back to the beginning of the meandering tale. I complied.

'The next morning Pete loaded a couple of local Himba men on the back of the *bakkie*, and off we went.'

'They must've been Zemba, not Himba,' Anthon interrupted again.

'What d'you mean, Zemba?' I asked, confused. 'I thought this area belonged to the Himba?'

'About two hundred years ago the Zemba tribe negotiated with the Himba for ownership of the land surrounding Ruacana. They're nomadic pastoralists like the Himba, but they speak an entirely different language. The Himba speaks Otjiherero.'

'Now you've taught me something,' I admitted.

'Anyway, they knew where the best stone could be found. The place I pointed out to you just now was our first stop. Pete drove off the road and into the veldt. We all got out of the vehicle and he and his men started to collect interesting rocks into a heap. I took the chance to walk around with my camera. The soil was ochre red and still damp from the previous night's storm. Gunther called me to come and look at something. On his hand was a tiny creature, looking like a tick or a fat bellied spider, except it was velvety and carmine red.'

'Ah!' Anthon exclaimed, 'a red velvet mite. They usually appear after the rain.'

'Yep,' I confirmed, 'and they're completely harmless. I've since read their wonderful colour is a defence mechanism. It warns any prospective predators that it tastes awful. After Gunther showed it to me, I noticed they were all over the place. I had to be careful not to crush them under my feet.'

'And the rocks? Could you use them?' Anthon asked. I gathered the falls were getting closer.

'The men collected quite a variety, but none of them were suitable as building stone. They were rounded and reddish brown in colour, but their surfaces were covered with a deep oxidation layer. Pete showed me that once scratched, the layer below was light orange. He explained it would've been difficult to build with them, they scarred far too easily. Of course, the men couldn't understand what the problem was. I noticed that they were muttering amongst themselves. Then one of them came up to us and said to Pete, in Afrikaans: "*Tate Kuru, hoekom hou die Meme nie van ons krippe nie?*'" which could be roughly translated as "Mister, why does the lady not *rike* the *locks*?'" He turned to the pile of rocks he and his fellow tribesmen had collected and waved his arms in exasperation. "*Wat's verkeerd met ons krippe?*" (What's *wlong* with our *locks*?) He turned towards Pete again, careful not to look in my direction. "*Die Meme wou krippe sien. Ons wys vir haar goeie krippe."* (The lady wanted to see *locks*. We showed her good *locks*.) Throwing his arms into the air, he ended with *"Krippe is tog krippe?"* (Are *locks* not *locks*?)'

Anthon hit the steering wheel with his hands as he boomed with laughter. 'How did you handle that?'

'I felt so sorry for the men, collecting all those rocks in the hot sun. I took the time to explain to them why the rocks, although good, wouldn't have withstood the journey to Oshakati and the construction process without losing their pristine quality. With Pete's help, we also explained where the rocks would be used. The idea that their home turf was chosen to provide the building materials for such an important structure fired them up. They all wanted to outdo each other with suggestions about where the search should head to next.'

'We spent the rest of the day driving to various sites. At one place, while we walked around scouting, we heard muffled explosions not far from where we were. Pete looked at Gunther. "Did I mention old Hendrik is around?" he said to him. "De-mining again?" Gunther asked casually, as if he just wanted to know what the weather was like. "What do you mean, de-mining?" I asked. I assumed I might've heard incorrectly. "Oh, nothing much," Pete answered, unperturbed. "Hendrik had gotten the contract to search for landmines planted during the Border War. When he finds one, he explodes it. That's what we just heard." I looked at them in disbelief. "Are you telling me we're in an area where there could still be land mines?" I wasn't convinced they weren't pulling my leg again. "Possibly," Pete answered, "but highly unlikely. Hendrik is thorough. He cleaned this area a couple of days ago." Yes, all in a days work, I thought to myself.'

Anthon looked at me and shook his head. 'At least you can't say your life was boring, *Mein Schatz,*' he smiled. 'But tell me, did you eventually find any suitable stone?'

'We did, in the end. We settled for round red rocks, fairly similar to what the men initially gathered, but a bit harder. Unfortunately, we never got to use it.'

'Why?' Anthon asked, surprised.

'Pete carted a truckload of rocks to Oshakati with which he built a sample wall for us to approve at the next site meeting. We didn't contend with the client's Very Clever Project Manager. An accountant, he was appointed as their financial coordinator but was of the opinion that he was also in charge of design, specification and construction. Unlike Pete and Gunther, he wasn't impressed with having to take instructions from a young smallish blonde female. I believe his brain was so infused with testosterone, it prevented him from applying these adjectives to the title of Architect. Initially he insisted that my sixty year old male boss also attend site meetings, but he tactfully managed to develop an irrefutable excuse shortly before every meeting. That allowed me to just get on with it.'

'Our Very Clever Project Manager didn't like the idea of natural stone. In his opinion it would make this Very Important Government Building look like a lodge. He insisted on getting a quotation to replace all natural stone on the project with large panels of polished marble. Imported from Italy, of course. We eventually managed to reach a compromise and settled for unpolished granite slabs, from the Karibib area. At least the product was Namibian.'

'Did this not cost a fortune?' Anthon asked.

'Of course it did. But fortunately it was his job to report back to his own Board of Directors. He was so desperate to effect this change, he managed to persuade them to allow the increase in cost. Gunther smiled all the way. Not only did his company score a massive client approved extra on the material, but they could also claim time cost, as it took much longer to get the granite on site. The upside of the matter was, we had heaps of red Ruacana rocks available for landscaping. Our landscape designer had a ball. He could cover most of the white *oshana* sand between his clusters of indigenous trees and succulents with ochre boulders.'

Chapter 4

OMAJOWA AT HIPPO POOLS

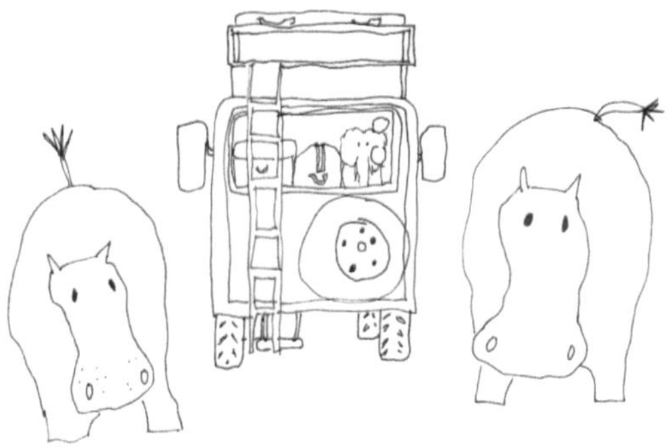

We reached the turnoff to the Ruacana Falls.

'Do you see that tiny building over there?' Anthon pointed to a rundown government structure, its faded grey walls pitted and pockmarked with small plaster craters. The entire area seemed deserted. We hadn't seen another vehicle since leaving Ruacana.

'The official Namibia-Angola border post. Those marks

are bullet holes. Still left from the war.' Yes, the war the old South African regime fought in northern Namibia, then South West Africa. A war to delay the inevitable, the passing of political power to the rightful citizens of Namibia. In my mind, as a hater of guns, war and most male testosterone games, the Border War was a senseless exercise. It sent countless young men to their death, or sentenced them to a life of disability, or an existence darkened by post-traumatic stress disorder. Families were ripped apart, wives widowed, children shipped off to the unknown. And the Powers Which Were 'outlawed' an entire country's right to say 'no'.

I chose to kill my shadowy train of thought and returned to the present.

'Surely we don't have to show our passports to get to the waterfall?' I panicked. I didn't have any documents with me.

'Not to worry,' Anthon reassured me, 'here we just walk around the border post. I'm not sure whether it's manned at the moment. If you happen to be a Zemba herdsman you move back and forth with your cattle as you please.'

As we rounded the structure, I became aware of a distant rumbling.

'The best view is from higher up,' Anthon advised, leading the way. I followed him, dazed by the heat, the screech of cicadas and the ever increasing drone of water. The pathway was dusty and overgrown, indicating not many people passed this way.

Without warning the vegetation lining our path cleared, revealing a thunderous avalanche of white froth tumbling into the gorge. We were nearly level with the top of the falls, separated from us by a narrow chasm more than 130m deep. Crawling onto a massive boulder protruding over the edge of the cliff, we pressed our bodies to the granite. The vibration penetrated my stomach and limbs until it seemed to reverberate in every cell of my body. We tried shouting and gesticulating but soon gave up. The sound was overwhelming, the spectacle magnificent.

Instead, I chose to immerse myself in the drama. My soul drifted along as the water cascaded over the edge of the cliff. The force of the fall vaporised the liquid, propelling the tiny molecules heavenwards again. Water droplets brushed my face, clung to my hair. Backlit by the lowering sun, the saffron mist outlined Anthon's profile with a squiggle of gold. I felt my camera pressing against my body, but somehow its lens couldn't capture the immensity of the experience.

'I hate to break this moment of utter perfection, *Mein Schatz*, but I think I hear our Omajowa screaming to be let out of Henry's drawer.' Anthon slid from our perch on the boulder, reaching out to help me down to the safety of the path. We still had to get to Hippo Pools and set up camp before sunset.

'This is what I love most about this part of Namibia,' I remarked. 'One stumbles upon these delightful scenic marvels without another soul around. No entrance fees, no flashing cameras, no fancy luxury hotels marring the landscape.'

'No concrete pathways and steel railings. No chips packets and chocolate wrappers and cooldrink bottles chucked into the bush.' Anthon added.

We walked back in silence, the volume of the rumble decreasing with each stride.

A blast of hot air struck us as we opened Henry's doors. We rolled down all our windows to allow a measure of air movement over our faces and bodies, then descended along the last stretch of road towards the river and Hippo Pools.

'Are there any hippos at the campsite?' I've been wondering about the name. We camped in a hippo path once before and I'd prefer not to make the same mistake again.

'There used to be many hippos in the Kunene, below the falls, but sadly, the last one was shot by someone from the Angolan side only last year. There are still many crocodiles, though,' Anthon replied.

'I guess that means we won't be swimming?' I sighed. Immersing one's body in a river of cool water sounded like heaven at that moment.

'I won't do any swimming, for sure,' Anthon answered. 'My Ruacana friends told me a story about a massive croc which used to dwell in the depths right under the falls. One year a family of Portuguese tourists passed this way, on their way from Angola to Oshakati. They camped here, at Hippo Pools. It was hot, as now. Grandpa took the kids to play in the shallow water on that sandbank, over there,' he pointed to a large shallow area on the side of the river, where the water appeared to be less than a metre deep. The white sand was visible through the clear water.

'He stood in the centre, while his grandchildren arranged themselves in a circle some distance around him. They played that game where he had to throw the ball at each kid in turn. He was no more than hip deep in the water. The next moment he disappeared under the surface, never to be seen again. The story goes that the giant croc passed between the kids, took the old man and dragged him back to his lair under the falls.'

'And nobody saw the croc?' I asked with a shudder.

'Nobody. And they never found his body or any trace of him,' Anthon concluded the macabre tale.

'Okay, you've persuaded me. I won't go swimming either.'

'There are rudimentary showers at the campsite though,' Anthon gave me the good news. 'We can cool down with a nice cold shower of river water before dinner.'

Arriving at the campsite, there was no sign of life at the wattle and daub hut guarding the open entrance gate.

'We normally just find a place we like and set up camp. The old Zemba *meme* who looks after the place will come and find us when it suits her. Come, I'll take you to my favourite spot.'

Stretched out along the bank of the river, the camping area is contained by a steep incline towards the escarpment. Huge Mopane trees create welcome shade for weary travellers. We stopped at the last campsite, where the river's edge and the now sheer rock embankment met each other. It was protected by a few massive Mopane trees, one of which clung precariously to the river bank while half its roots were suspended dramatically over the water. Indeed a lovely place to spend the night.

After a life saving cool shower, we set up camp. To open the rooftop tent and prepare the bed took five minutes. To unpack our canvas chairs and folding table took two.

'I guess we only need the cotton kikois to sleep under?' I asked as I unpacked the pillows in the hot tent.

'Definitely,' Anthon replied. 'It might get a bit cooler when the west-wind wafts up the river, usually early morning, but it won't be cold.'

'Shall I open all the flaps then?' I asked.

'I'll roll up the canvass coverings from outside,' he

answered. 'Open the inner flaps, but keep the gauze zipped down. Before you come down the ladder, spray the inside of the tent with that Death to Flying Insects stuff we bought this afternoon, then zip down the entrance gauze as well. That way we should be insect free for the night.'

After spraying myself with the mosquito repellant and lighting a citronella candle on the camp table, I joined Anthon on one of the sturdy Mopane roots, projecting over the river. He offered me a gin and tonic. Ice cubes, courtesy of Jeannie, clinked seductively against the side of the glass. A slice of cucumber added a splash of green.

'Just to make up for the shebeen's version, *Mein Schatz*.'

'What a privilege,' I sighed, as I made myself comfortable. 'I can see why this is your favourite spot.'

We were about three meters above the water. The steep river bank precluded any danger of a crocodile finding its way into our camp. The sun, engorged and distorted like a crimson balloon, was about to crash into the river; its final fiery shriek skimming off the mirror smooth Kunene, dusting our faces with a reddish-gold brush. As the last flame of copper finally drowned, a faint chirping became audible, growing louder and louder. As it reached a crescendo, a wave of tiny birds appeared from behind us. They swished and surged, in perfect unison, like a school of small fish; a curling, dancing shadow against the rosy sky, finally landing with a chattering sigh in the reeds on the opposite river bank. Just as we thought it was over, the next wave arrived. Then another. And another. And yet another. For at least twenty minutes, as dusk fell over the quiet river, the birds kept on coming; gracefully surging through the sky like ghosts. We sat in complete silence. I could feel my inner rhythm synching with the pulse of the earth.

'Red-billed Queleas. They must feel safe on the island,' Anthon finally dared to break the spell.

'It's an island?' My body plucked my soaring soul back to the present, to where we sat, suspended over the river.

'Yep,' he answered. 'We're on the bank of the smaller channel. The main river passes on the other side.' He left our seat and started to pack a few pieces of firewood onto the small concrete platform provided for that purpose.

'Time to prepare dinner. My stomach is rumbling.'

Soon a healthy fire gyrated against a tourist brochure backdrop of perfectly still water reflecting the last radiance of the day.

'To win first prize for the most kitsch picture ever, I'll command the moon to pop out from behind that mountain, over there,' Anthon pointed at the peak across the river, 'just about ... NOW!' We looked at each other and burst out laughing as the unsuspecting culprit gently soared out from behind the mountain he pointed to.

'You cheated!' I tried to hit him on his arm, but he danced away, holding the now fully opened Omajowa as shield in front of him.

'I didn't cheat,' he quipped, 'I saw the glimmer of the moon behind that mountain peak and read the signs. Now let me show you how to prepare the most delicious fungus on the planet.'

With a small knife, he commenced removing the crusty layer which covered the dome.

'Be careful to keep the head horizontal when you do this. You don't want any of the grit or sand to lodge into the fins,' he explained. Next, he cut the stalk flush with the underside, putting the cleaned white disk on a plate, covering its entire surface.

'I'm going to clean the stalk as well; the peel comes off easily with a sharp knife,' he continued. 'Now come and feel the difference in texture between the top and the stem.'

I touched the silky smooth skin of the mushroom's head, squeezing it lightly between my thumb and middle finger, repeating it with the stalk. 'The stalk is much firmer and appears to be drier and coarser than the head,' was my verdict.

'Exactly; the stalk can last much longer as well. I'm therefore going to wrap it in a paper bag and put it in the Engel. It should last until we get back to Windhoek. Perhaps I can persuade the boys to join us for dinner one evening. They love Omajowa.' His voice became wistful.

Anthon fetched the pan we borrowed from Jeannie.

'When she heard we'll be cooking Omajowa, she also gave me a leek and a bit of nutmeg.' He proceeded to slice the mushroom into thick slices, which he then cut in half to fit into the pan. 'My friend Albie makes the most wonderful Omajowa Schnitzel.' He loves chattering away as he cooked. 'Albie has a pan large enough to take the entire head. He first dunks it in flour, then in beaten egg, repeating the process if it doesn't stick properly; then he fries it in a good amount of butter until it's golden brown.' By this time our pan, a large chunk of butter melting in it, was heating on a few hot coals which Anthon had scratched to the side. 'But the way we'll have it tonight is still my favourite,' he continued. 'Simple. Fried in butter, with a thinly sliced leek, salt and pepper and a grinding of fresh nutmeg. Delicious.'

Soon after, the unique aroma of butter, leeks and Omajowa filled the air.

'This will be our starter.' Anthon put the pan in the middle of the camping table, then added more wood to the fire. I lit a candle; our plates, cutlery and wine glasses long since waiting on the table over which an extra kikoi was draped earlier. He fetched the wine from the Engel; an ice cold bottle of South African Chenin.

'Cheers, *Mein Schatz,* thanks for sharing this with me.' He lifted his glass while his eyes held mine, serious, for a change. Crystal upon crystal pierced the quiet darkness, the movement stirring the candle flame ever so slightly.

'Thanks for giving me the opportunity to share this with you,' I answered.

We ate in silence, savouring every delicious morsel, pausing only to take another sip of the crisp wine.

Once the entire Omajowa had disappeared, we sat back in our canvas chairs, drinking our wine while watching the moon, now high above the mountains.

'For our main course, we'll be having *as-wors* and *braaibroodjies,*' Anthon informed me.

A *braaibroodjie* is a local favourite. Literally translated from the Afrikaans, it means 'grilled bread.' A sandwich is made with cheese, preferably a matured cheddar, tomatoes and onions. I love to spread mayonnaise on the one side, Anthon prefers chutney. I butter the inside, some people believe you must butter the outside. This goes on a grid and is then toasted over hot coals. Not too hot, though, or you'll end up with charcoaled *braaibroodjies*. What makes them so special is the smokiness added by the wood fire.

'What do you mean by *as-wors*?' I asked. Although my mother tongue is Afrikaans, I've never heard the term before.

'It's the best way ever to cook *boerewor*s on a fire.'

'Why?' I asked. '*As* means ash. Why would you want your sausage to be full of ash?'

'I hope not full of ash, *Mein Schatz,* just grilled directly on the coals, without a grid. Let me show you.' He shovelled the burning pieces of wood to one side, spreading the red hot coals into a deep even layer.

'Firstly you've got to get hold of really good quality thick sausage as this *boerewors* Jeannie packed for us.' Here I must explain that the term *boerewors* can be directly translated as farmers' sausage. In South Africa and Namibia, it denotes a fairly wide variety of old family recipes, each claiming to be the ultimate way to make it.

'I normally break the round of *boerewors* into shorter pieces, otherwise it's impossible to turn. Like this,' he divided the length of sausage into pieces roughly twenty centimetres long, 'which you lay directly onto the searing hot coals. When they start to sizzle, you turn them over, with a pair of tongs, if you remembered to pack them… Dammit! It's hot!' He used his fingers, the tongs were obviously still in Windhoek. 'Take the sausage off the coals no more than two minutes later…' this time he used a fork, lifting the still sizzling sausage onto a plate, '…and *voilá*! You've got the most succulent *as-wors* ever.'

'It sure looks great!' My mouth watered. 'Sausage must be underdone and juicy,' I added. 'There are few things worse than a piece of dry, overcooked meat.'

'Let's eat this first.' Anthon put the plate on the table, fetched our wine from the Engel and refilled our glasses. When it was cool enough to handle, I picked up an entire piece with my hand and took a bite. I felt the warm juice dribbling down the side of my mouth, over my chin and onto my shorts.

'Orgasmic! As our dear Nanna would say,' I said, licking the last drops from my fingers.

'And d'you know what?' Anthon added, 'this never tastes as nice if you make it at home. You need to be in an awesome location, preferably far from civilisation.'

After the *as-wors*, I was sated; for the time being, anyway. The *braaibroodjies* would have to wait another half an hour or so. I sat with my wine glass in front of me, idly observing a huge moth drawn to our table by the candlelight. Velvety brown, with large black eye-like circles on its lower wings, I held out my finger for it to land on. Soft and powdery, it was larger than my outstretched hand.

'You're holding the mother of a Mopane caterpillar on your hand,' Anthon joked. 'We might see some further south, tomorrow.'

My attention shifted to a couple of mosquitos spiralling close to the candle's flame.

'Aren't you worried about us getting malaria, it being summer and rainy season?' I asked.

'Not really,' Anthon replied. 'There are many misconceptions about how one contracts the disease. I believe the first and best line of defence is still protection. If all households in northern Namibia and the Caprivi can be persuaded to sleep under undamaged nets, instead of using them for illegal fishing, we'll have only a few cases of malaria every year.'

'But what about us sitting here, right now?' I asked, 'we're not sitting under a net?'

'That's the interesting part,' Anthon explained. 'Malaria is only carried by the female Anopheles mosquito, which is active between about eleven in the evening and four in the morning.'

'Sounds like an old woman's tale to me,' I sniggered.

'Not at all,' Anthon replied. 'The life cycle of the Plasmodium falciparum, which is the predominant malaria parasite in Namibia, is the key to the time of day the infection takes place. The infection cycle is synchronised, which means more or less all the parasites in the blood will be at the same stage of development in the red blood cells where they multiply. The amazing thing is, this clocking mechanism of the parasite is dependent on the human host's own circadian rhythm.'

'You've lost me. Repeat in language which an architect can understand,' I protested.

He laughed, then explained with all the patience of a teacher: 'The malaria parasite reproduces in red blood cells. Patients who've got malaria develop their worst symptoms late afternoon and early evening, with severe fever from around eight till twelve in the evening. This happens because the red blood cells filled with malaria parasites burst and release the highest concentration of parasites into the blood at this time of day. It's therefore vital for the parasite's survival that its other host, the mosquito, will feed at the time when it's most likely to ingest the maximum number of parasites. That means between eleven at night and four in the morning.'

'Wow! Incredible!' I was impressed with the ingenuity of nature.

'Therefore,' he continued, 'if, for safety's sake, you protect yourself from being bitten from dusk till dawn by using an effective mosquito repellant and covering your body with clothing…' —here I glanced guiltily at my own bare arms and legs. At least I sprayed copious amounts of mozzie repellant all over them — '…and sleep under a net or inside a tent, your chances of contracting malaria are slim.'

'So that's why I had to spray the tent with that horrible stuff before I closed it up?' I asked.

'Yes, the insecticide should kill any mosquitos lurking inside, meaning we should sleep without being bitten,' he confirmed.

'So do you never advise your patients to take prophylaxis?' I asked.

'That's an incorrect assumption. When tourists from outside of Namibia, especially from Europe or the US, tell me they plan to visit these parts, particularly in summer, I always advise them to protect themselves as well as take the most recently developed prophylaxis. Provided they take it strictly according to the instructions. However, with my local patients, my advice is usually to protect rather than medicate.'

'Why the difference in advice?' I kept on digging

'Most European clinics want a positive malaria test as well as see the parasites in the blood sample before they'll consider treatment,' Anthon explained. 'In some cases, it may be too late. To give you a few statistics: There are different types of malaria parasites on the planet. In our part of the world, the most common is Plasmodium falciparum. It's also the deadliest species of all of them and responsible for about 50 per cent of all malaria deaths worldwide. 91 per cent of malaria deaths occur in Africa, mostly children under the age of five. It kills roughly 1 million people every year. Plasmodium falciparum is also the parasite which can cause cerebral malaria, which doesn't wait for positive tests before it kills you. I prefer to treat the patient, not the negative malaria test. There are other parameters one can look at in blood tests, which change before the test shows positive. This is especially important in the treatment of patients with chronic or recurrent malaria.'

'Recurrent malaria? So it's true once you've been infected you can get the illness again and again?' I asked.

'Definitely,' Anthon continued. 'With chronic and recurrent malaria the test more often than not shows negative. Come to think of it, I've got a couple of patients with the condition. Some time ago I received a phone call from one of them. "Doc," he said, "I'm in a taxi on my way to Hamburg Airport. I've just discharged myself from the Institute for Tropical Diseases. I've tried for forty-eight hours to explain to these fucking clever doctors I've got recurrent malaria, but as I'd tested negative and they couldn't see the damn parasites in my blood, they refused to treat me. Please just book me a hospital bed. I land at six am."'

'This guy had been working here in Northern Namibia for many years. He'd had at least nine previous bouts of malaria. He knew his symptoms and his body better than any test or doctor. In those days we still treated malaria with intravenous quinine, so the patient had to be admitted to hospital. I had no doubt if he believed he had malaria, it was definitely the case, so I went ahead and booked the bed immediately. He was only well enough to be discharged ten days later.' Anthon paused to take a sip of wine.

'So what I'm in effect saying to you is most experienced Namibian doctors know what malaria looks like. Once I've got the patient's history and know where they've been, depending on their condition, I might start treatment before the test shows positive. People die of malaria, *Mein Schatz*.'

'Have you ever lost a patient that way?' I asked.

'Yes.' His eyes became serious. 'The first patient I ever lost as a private practitioner was due to malaria.'

'Want to tell me what happened?'

He got up, fetched a cigarette and walked over to the huge old Mopane tree on the river bank. Leaning against the trunk, he dangled the cigarette between his fingers.

'A young couple from Mozambique stopped by my surgery. They were travelling through Namibia with their two children, spent some time in Etosha and were on their way back home. The woman didn't feel well and wanted me to give her a prescription for malaria tablets, as she thought she might've contracted the disease. After examining her I realised she was already seriously ill and needed urgent hospitalisation. When I suggested this, she refused. She insisted the tablets should suffice and would allow her to get home, to Mozambique. I replied I could under no circumstances give her the prescription as it would be irresponsible. I urged her to allow me to admit her to hospital immediately and put her on intravenous malaria treatment. I told her she'd have to go to another doctor, should she insist on the tablets.' He stopped talking, finally lighting the cigarette.

'And?'

Anthon shook his head as he watched the cigarette smoke twirl into the low hanging branches.

'She initially refused to go to hospital, but her husband eventually persuaded her to listen to me. By the time she was admitted, she was really ill. I called a colleague, a specialist physician, and together we did all we could, but we couldn't save her. She passed away forty-eight hours later.'

'How long had you been in private practice by then?' I asked.

'Four, maybe five years,' he replied. Then he looked at

me, his eyes questioning, distressed: 'You know, *Mein Schatz,* when we're young we face life, our professions, full of bravado. We shall succeed where our parents failed. We shall save the world, make life better for every patient crossing our path. When you see a patient die, and you realise you're completely powerless, that you couldn't prevent them dying, you're all of a sudden confronted with your own vulnerability and your own limitations as a human, as a doctor.'

Chapter 5

KISSING A CROCODILE

The candle vibrated purple and yellow as a mosquito disappeared into its flame. Returning from where he leant against the Mopane tree, Anthon flicked his cigarette butt into the campfire.

'Ready for the last course?' he walked towards the coals, now not half as red as when he grilled the sausage. He held his open hand over them to test the heat, then scratched a few hot embers, still glowing bright red, from under the last pieces of burning wood. 'I'll have to do the *braaibroodjies* now, before the coals are too cold.'

I helped him to pack the bread onto the small grid. Suddenly he stood upright, listening intently.

'Did you hear that?' he said as he grabbed the torch, taking me by the hand and leading me to the edge of the river bank. I heard nothing beyond the night song of cicadas and frogs. In the moonlight, the river ran dark and deep. Then my ears picked up a soft 'plonk' as if a small creature had just jumped into the stream. He shone the torch in the direction of the noise, the yellow beam cutting a wedge into the black water. Two small eyes glittered red.

'What is it?' I whispered.

'A baby crocodile,' he replied.

Straining my eyes I could make out the shape of the smallish reptile. Anthon slowly moved the spot of light, revealing more crocs floating in the river.

'Did I ever tell you how we kissed the baby crocodiles?' he asked, back to his old self; eyes twinkling mischievously in the firelight.

'Kissing crocs? Not that I can recall?'

'Perhaps I shouldn't tell you this story,' he teased, 'it's not one I'm particularly proud of.'

'I know you'll tell it anyway.'

'In my defence, it took place when things were really bad at home, quite a while before I met you.'

'And things got even worse,' I added, chuckling.

He put the grid on the coals, keeping the torch handy while he stood watching the sandwiches. *Braaibroodjies* must be toasted to a crisp golden brown, not burned black.

'Come on, get going with your story,' I urged.

'I regarded these trips as essential for my sanity,' he began. 'I often camped down here by myself.'

'Drop the excuses. Get to the embarrassing part.' I knew full well these trips allowed him to think, to listen to music, to try and make sense of his life, of everything.

'You know how I love my long stories. You can only hear about the embarrassing part if you're prepared to listen to the entire saga,' he feigned indignation, swiping in my direction with the dishcloth.

'I concede!' I shouted, raising my arms in surrender.

'It was also summer, but October or November. That terrible time of year when the heat is relentless. The rainy season usually only starts in late December. It was so hot that I opened all the tent flaps, just keeping the gauze zipped closed. After taking a cold shower, I collapsed on a damp towel, stark naked. Spread out like a starfish, straight on my back. I made sure no two body parts touched each other. This was extremely tricky; for obvious reasons,' he chuckled.

'Sometimes friends from Ruacana joined me. A couple of them have boats and love to come down here for a *braai* and a bit of fishing. Of course, these guys never *braai* or fish without the necessary refreshments. And here we're talking copious amounts of beer, whiskey, brandy and coke, you name it. They believed drinking water when they were thirsty could be bad for their health,' he jested.

By now the *braaibroodjies* were ready. We sat down at the table once more, each with a piping hot toast on which dark grooves demarcated the lines where it had been seared by the grid. Melted cheese oozed from between the bread halves. We shared the last few drops of wine.

'Anyway, on this particular day Dries and Neels decided I needed company. Dries brought his boat down. It was wonderful to experience this rugged part of the world from the water. One rarely encounters other people. We must've been the only boat on the river for the next fifty miles. Except for a couple of Angolan fisherman in their *makoros*.'

—A *makoro* is a wooden dugout canoe, carved from a single log. It's propelled forward by a man standing in the stern, pushing it through the shallows with a pole.—

Anthon bit into the toast, cheese dripping onto the plate in front of him.

'The day was terrific. I hadn't had so much fun in years. Didn't have so much to drink in a long time either. Late afternoon we started the fire, here in this exact spot. As the sun went down, a lamb rib and a couple of T-bone steaks were sizzling on the coals.'

'Did you have anything else to eat that day?' I asked, although I already knew the answer.

'*Biltong* and *droë wors*,' he laughed. The Namibian and South African staple. Spiced, cured and air-dried beef, game and sausage.

'You know these guys, *Mein Schatz*, they survive on meat and drink. Ask any Namibian farmer what he eats for vegetables and his answer would be pork and chicken.' His roar of laughter stirred some of the birds on the island into a chirpy flutter. He took a bite of his toast, then fetched another bottle of wine.

I had the picture. An entire day on a boat in this heat, little to eat, lots of alcohol.

He filled our glasses.

'Once we'd finished all the meat and most of the liquid refreshments, as Dries called it, Neels asked me, "Doc, have you ever kissed a crocodile?" I told him I've never been drunk or lonely enough to want to kiss one, why did he want to know? Without answering me, he looked at Dries. "Dries," he said, "don't you agree what our Doc needs is to kiss a crocodile?"'

'"Wait a minute, I'm not that desperate," I told them, "I

might be having a hard time at the moment, but I'm not ready to commit suicide just yet." They'd hear none of it. Dries was suddenly all fired up with this new idea. "Doc," he announced, "we'll choose a baby croc for you to kiss. We won't hurt it, I promise." As if I could care at that stage whether the freaking croc would be hurt. But once they'd hatched this idea, there was no way to persuade them otherwise. "It's pitch dark out there. How are we going to find these baby crocs?" I asked, impressed with my own brilliance. "Don't you worry, Doc," Dries consoled me, "see the shimmer behind that mountain over there? The moon will soon be out."'

"That's how you knew," I interjected. Anthon hardly paused his narrative.

'If all else fails, we'll use this! On the word 'this', Neels switched on a massive portable spotlight. I swear we could've lit up that mountain with it,' Anthon continued while pointing at the same peak.

'Next thing they marched me down to the boat. I'd no idea what to expect, but at that moment I realised the easiest route would be to go with the flow. Once on board, Dries started the engine, then turned it right down to a near drift. Neels sat in front, shining the spotlight on the water. The first set of red eyes we met were rather far apart. "Nope," Neels shook his head, "too big." Just as I considered feeling relieved, Neels's light reflected off a smaller pair. "Dries!" he yelled, "cut the engine!" Dries throttled the engine, allowing the boat to drift towards the reptile. Mesmerised by the light, it made no attempt to move away. "Now show Doc how to do it!" Without waiting for a second invitation, Dries hung over the side, legs hooked under the bench for stability. His upper body and arms were swinging freely over the river. Neels kept the beam of light on the croc. At the exact moment the reptile was within reach, Dries swooped down towards the water and grabbed it by the snout with a "Come to mama, my baby." Closing both hands tightly around its schnozzle, he lifted it out of the water and kissed it on the lips. Before the creature could even contemplate defending itself by lashing at its captor with its tail, Dries allowed it to slide back into the water. The entire performance appeared so effortless and elegant that I needed no persuasion to try it as well. After a couple of unsuccessful attempts, I was ready to give up. By this time Dries and Neels were just about paralytic with laughter, never mind alcohol. "Come on Doc," Dries urged me. "You can do this!" He was still talking when Neels shouted, "Here she is, Doc, she's been waiting for you all evening!" As Dries cut the engine, I saw it: the smallest, the minutest baby croc, floating towards us, its innocent eyes spellbound by the light. I hooked my legs under the bench and swung my torso overboard. At that moment all I saw were two glittering red eyes, much more frightened by the apparition it faced than I could ever be of it. I closed my hands around its tiny snout and kissed it full on the lips. Then a strange emotion washed over me; I just couldn't bear to part with it! I wanted to keep on holding it, loving it. "Drop it Doc!" Dries screamed, "Listen to me, drop it! NOW!" Pain seared along my arm.'

Anthon stood there, rubbing his left arm, as though the painful experience was still in progress.

'The little shit slapped me with its tail! I let go of the reptile, dropping the poor creature from much higher than Dries and Neels ever did; but it was in self-defence!'

'Extraordinary,' I laughed.

'What?' he replied, feigning shock, hands turned

outwards and upwards in a gesture implying complete innocence.

'Men,' I said. 'When you combine alcohol and testosterone, you get away with murder.'

'No, *Mein Schatz,* not murder. True to Dries' promise, no animals were hurt during the enactment of this story.' He boomed with laughter at his own ingenuity.

'Except for yourself, of course.' I joined in the mirth as I got my own back.

By now all that was left of the fire was a smouldering heap of embers. I blew out the candle. Melting into my camping chair, I folded my hands behind my head and looked up at the sky. The Milky Way was slowly being devoured by darkness drifting in from the east. Anthon followed my gaze.

'I think we're in for a bit of rain tonight,' he remarked. 'It's clouding over.'

'Probably a good idea to pack everything into Henry,' I agreed, 'and tuck in for the night.'

Just as well we did. As we zipped up our tent flap, the rain came down. Cool air washed away the oppressive heat. I was lulled to sleep by the echoing of thunder between the distant mountains, too far to be of concern to me as I dreamed of floating down a benign cool river, free of crocodiles, drunken men on boats and other dangerous creatures.

We woke at dawn. Getting out of the tent, our surroundings appeared untouched by humans, the sand surrounding Henry smooth and fresh after the rain.

'Let's have an early start while it's still cool,' Anthon suggested, fetching the gas cooker and the coffee percolator.

'I vote for having a shower first. Then we can fetch water for the coffee at the same time and save Henry's for the trip through the desert.' I collected our towels and a bottle of soap. The ablution block was a short walk from our campsite. We had to search for the pathway through the lush vegetation. Everything was wet with rain. As we walked, hundreds of minute spider eyes glimmered on silky, dew decorated webs spun between the grass. Eager to get to the shower first, I rushed ahead, swinging a long stick in front of me to remove the strands of silk barring my way. I entered the small reed shelter, by now brightly lit by the sun.

'Oh my God!' I screamed as I stretched my hand towards the tap.

'If it's a snake, just freeze!' Anthon shouted from behind, ever the level headed protector.

'No, it's not a snake, it's a creature from a Harry Potter film.' By now I was over my initial shock. The most bizarre spider I'd ever seen, sat in the middle of the basin. Its body was triangular, its leg-span nearly as big as my outstretched hand.

'I've got to fetch my camera to photograph it,' I said, 'otherwise the girls won't believe me.' I turned to Anthon. 'Please don't kill it while I'm gone. If you leave it alone it won't harm you.'

'You know I'm not fond of spiders,' he mumbled from a safe distance, then closely scrutinised every corner of the shower cubicle for similar monsters.

'Not afraid to kiss a crocodile, but scared to death of anything with eight legs,' I teased. 'Come, let's shower first. If we don't disturb it, it won't go anywhere. I'll come back with my camera while you make coffee.'

After a refreshing cold shower, I returned to take a few photographs. By the time I got back to our camp, the coffee was ready. We huddled together on the Mopane tree root over the river, savouring our coffee and a couple of rusks.

'I don't want to leave,' I said. 'This spot is so special.'

'In an hour from now, when the sun starts to bake, you'll quickly change your tune,' he replied as he chased me up. 'I'll go and find the *Meme* in charge of the campsite and pay her.'

While he was away I washed our cups and packed the last few items.

'We must come back. I want us to drive west along the Kunene to Swartbooisdrift,' I said when he returned.

'Telepathy, *Mein Schatz*,' he answered. 'Walking back here I had a brilliant idea. Why don't we bring Nic and Alex on a camping trip during the May school holidays?' Another excursion was born. No wonder our kids joked we spent most of our time planning the next meal or the next trip.

Soon we were on our way back to Ruacana where we dropped the pan with Jeannie. From there Anthon turned Henry's nose towards Opuwo on a road resembling a rolled out ribbon of white mud after the previous night's storm. The slush sprayed and splattered Henry's body, transforming his back and sides into Jackson Pollock masterpieces. For some distance we drove through woodland. The leaves on the trees were washed unusually green by the rain. Normally it was caked with white dust churned up by passing vehicles. Rounding a bend, the road stretched out in front of us over a low Mopane covered plain, for as far as we could see.

'From here one drive straight for a stretch of 110km,' Anthon informed me.

'Surely you didn't measure it?' I laughed, assuming he was indulging in a bit of statistical exaggeration.

'Of course I did,' he replied, delighted with himself. 'I drove this road by myself so often, I had to find ways to pass the time.'

We slipped into silence. The endless landscape of white dust and Mopane scrub, the unswerving road, Henry's sing-song, all conspired to pull me into the whirlpool connecting awareness to the dream world.

'Look at all the Mopane worms!' The excitement in Anthon's voice tore me out of my trance.

'Where? What?' Pulling myself upright in the seat I strained my eyes against the bright light, the fuzz in my brain refusing to recognise anything matching the word 'Mopane worm'.

'The entire road is covered with them,' he cried.

I refocused, concentrating on the gravel surface visible over Henry's spare tyre, fitted onto the bonnet. The white dust was streaked with black squiggles as the plump creatures wriggled across it. We were driving on a carpet of caterpillars.

'Just like humans. Those in the west want to be in the east,' Anthon shook his head.

'Can't we stop for a bit?' I begged, 'I'd love to take a few close-ups.'

He brought Henry to a halt on the side of the road, while I searched for my camera. Behind us, two tracks of squashed Mopane worms stretched into the distance. Anthon held up his hand.

'Shhhh. Do you hear it?'

'Hear what?' I whispered, not sure whether I was allowed to talk audibly.

'How they chew! Listen!'

Once my brain registered what I was hearing, I broke

into laughter. The air was thick with the crunchy sound of millions of minute jaws gnawing away at the Mopane leaves.

I walked into the veldt with my camera and pointed its lens at a striking specimen creeping along a low Mopane branch. It was fat and velvety black, sprinkled with spiky yellow and red candy. Its tiny head moved up and down in its search for another butterfly shaped leaf to devour.

'Mopane worms are a favourite Oshivambo delicacy,' Anthon informed me. 'They prefer them to be dried or smoked. Remember those baskets filled with all sorts of interesting foods we saw at the market in Oshakati?'

'Have you ever eaten any?' I asked. 'What do they taste like?'

'Only once. To me it tasted like rubber. But then I must admit, I didn't enjoy oysters the first time either, yet now I adore them. The worms are often cooked with tomatoes, chillies and onions; incredibly high in protein. Some experts are of the opinion the Mopane worm, if harvested with care, can feed Africa.'

My pictures taken, I brushed my finger along the rippling length of my photographic subject. Its cool body felt silky soft.

'Can you see how certain Mopane shrubs are nearly stripped bare of leaves, but others seem to be ignored by the caterpillars?' I recalled a snippet of trivia I picked up somewhere. 'The Mopane tree has a rather ingenious way of protecting itself against hungry animals. The tree senses when it's threatened, when too many leaves are harvested, then gives off a turpentine-like scent which warns the rest of the herd to leave it alone.'

'Clever,' Anthon agreed.

'What would this be?' I asked, my attention drawn to a coffee coloured lump hanging between two sticks.

'It's a cocoon,' he answered. 'Have you ever seen woven Mopane silk?'

'So this is where the silk comes from?' I was amazed. 'One of the shops at the Windhoek Craft Gallery sells scarves woven with the raw silk; expensive, but exquisite.' Something to add to my collection in future. When my budget allows.

As the midday sun scorched through a gap between the clouds, we rushed back to the shady comfort of Henry and drove further over the wriggling mass on the white road. The African sun isn't to be taken lightly at any time of day, especially in summer.

We continued our journey along the road without an end.

Chapter 6

ANATOMY AND A FAMILY

'Why did you choose medicine as a career?'

I'm fascinated by Anthon's stories. We can talk for hours on end, turning these long journeys into a smorgasbord of anecdotes and life histories intertwined with the most awe-inspiring scenery imaginable. When the sound system decides to play along, a soundtrack of lofty music elevates the experience to divine.

'Why? Because it's in the nature of things I should be

one, I suppose,' his voice giving away that another profession never even made a possible list of career choices.

'I always knew I wanted to be a medical doctor one day.'

'But you grew up on a farm in the Kalahari?' I probed. 'Isn't it normal for a farm boy to want to follow in his father's footsteps and become a farmer?'

'Have you ever regarded me as normal?' He burst out laughing.

'No,' I conceded.

'As for becoming a farmer, there's a real reason why I never even considered it.' Did I detect a cloud brushing over his Joker Persona?

A lone pickup truck appeared in the distance, grew larger and larger, then stormed past. The still damp road hardly burped a whiff of white dust.

'But let's get back to why I wanted to be a doctor.' The jovial storyteller again.

'I loved dissecting creatures. Dead ones, of course,' he chuckled. 'Growing up on a farm taught me to keep myself busy. I had the freedom to roam where I wanted to, often barefoot; my two dogs were my protectors. I was incredibly inquisitive. I had to know how everything worked, but where most kids would've been happy to take their father's electric razor apart, I wanted to know how living things were put together.'

'Was that the reason why you sometimes messed up your mother's kitchen?' I teased. 'She never told me the full episode?'

'*That* story,' he grinned. 'She loves to tell everybody that old *Geschichte*.' (The German word for story, or history, as he intended here.)

'Apparently, I found a dead tortoise in the veldt when I

was a toddler. According to my mother, I wasn't yet four years old. I brought the carcass home and proceeded to dissect it with one of her carving knives. Right there, on the kitchen table.'

'Sounds like the sort of thing boys do?' I grew up with two brothers.

'Except normally the tortoise wouldn't have been lying dead for how many days in the Kalahari sun. According to my mother's legend, its innards were short of dissolved into a rotten stinking liquid.'

'I think I get the picture.'

'By the time she discovered what I was up to, the revolting mess covered every conceivable kitchen surface, including my entire body, my hair, my clothing.'

'Yuk,' I shuddered. 'I imagine she also had the privilege to clean you up?'

'No ways, not *my* mother. She called my nanny and told her to put the old zinc bath on the lawn, then to fill it with the hosepipe and put me in it. With lots of soap.'

I laughed. 'You can't blame her. In the absence of a nanny, I would've put you on the lawn and hosed you down from a safe distance myself.'

'Next, I graduated to the carcasses of slaughtered farm animals,' he continued.

'I hope they were a bit fresher than the tortoise,' I snuck in. He ignored my comment.

'After removing the lungs, my father showed me how to pump them up to see what happens when they fill with air. I loved to hang around in the butchery when the meat was processed for the kitchen. I was fascinated with anatomy, with the inner workings of the body. How the muscles and tendons were fixed around the bones. How the knee and other joints allowed the limbs to move. What the different organs looked like and where they were located. Here I could experiment as much as I wanted to. At least I didn't make as much of a mess as with the tortoise, as these dissections took place in the *Biltongzimmer*.'

'Which is?' I asked.

'The biltong room. Every farmhouse in this part of the world has a room dedicated to the preparation and drying of biltong, but also used for making sausage or *Rauchfleish* (smoked meat), or all sorts of other cured delicacies.'

We slowed down for a herd of goats. They seemed intent on devouring every shoot of green as it appeared at the edge of the road.

'Tell me more about the farm,' I asked. 'Tell me about Eirup.'

His face softened, his expression was contemplative. 'Happy stories or sad stories?'

'Both. Whatever you're comfortable with.'

He doesn't carry baggage about his past. He never paints his family members and ancestors with a golden glow, just to put himself in a better light. He gives his compliments where they're due, but also describes people and events with ruthless honesty.

'Have you ever been into the Kalahari, east of Mariental?' he asked.

'Never. I've only driven past Mariental along the B1 on my way to Cape Town,' I replied.

'The Kalahari's got its own beauty,' he pinched his lower lip into a habitual upside down half-moon, as he visualised the landscapes of his childhood. He stared into the distance, far beyond the road in front of Henry.

'In the Kalahari, the veldt is wide. When the skies are

clear and there's no breeze, the blue is so overwhelming it wants to crush you into the earth. Then the wind starts to blow. Fat fluffy clouds drift in from the east, their tummies orangey-pink as their undersides reflect the red of the sand. Below, their dark shadows slink silently over the veldt, just like that artist you like so much, paints them.'

'Nicolaas Maritz?' I asked.

'Yep, he's got the ability to bare the soul of the Kalahari.' He took a deep breath, then continued:

'Although the landscape appears flat, in reality, it is corrugated. Dune upon red dune, covered with grass and Acacia trees, form parallel lines into the distance. Every now and again a pan appears. Here water collects in a good rain year into flat, shallow lakes; sometimes small, sometimes massive. There's one which attracts flocks of cerise pink flamingoes during exceptionally wet seasons. Others sprout lilies as if from nowhere. Game abounds; springbok, kudu, gemsbok, ostriches, jackal.'

He paused. Reaching for his cigarette packet, he shook one out, then lit it.

'On the farm, there was this special place I often escaped to. An entire forest of Camel Thorn trees. I always visualised how I'd one day build my house right there, a waterhole close enough to observe the game without disturbing them.'

'You make it sound like a paradise,' I said.

'It is,' he took a deep drag, allowing the smoke to twirl out of the window. 'But only when there's been enough rain to sustain every living thing relying on the land for sustenance. When the rains stayed away, and winter approached, one could feel the tension everywhere, whether in the morbid tone of the adults or the jittery behaviour of the animals. It's a schizophrenic, a bipolar part of the world to grow up in. The farms must be massive because the carrying capacity is so low. It's a beautiful, but brutal region to be a farmer in. Yet, once in your blood, it's achingly difficult to give it up.'

Although I've never lived on a farm, I also understand the deep attachment one develops to place, to the landscapes your life unfolded in.

Then again, you can't miss something you've never had. If one chooses a life rich in experience, filled with travel and time spent with special people, one must accept the inevitability of living with a certain type of sadness; of waking up some days with an inexplicable melancholy for a memory from long ago.

'You wanted to know why I didn't become a farmer?' His voice had a metallic edge, his mouth uncharacteristically severe, the Joker completely gone. He seemed in a trance, to have forgotten the cigarette end still balanced between his fingers.

'When I was about twelve, we were in the middle of a severe drought. My father handed me the keys to the *bakkie* and told me to drive out to the cattle posts, where we put out fodder for the animals next to the water troughs. "I want you to take your rifle along," he said to me. "Get out of the bakkie at the post and walk up to the springbok lying under the trees. If an animal doesn't get up and run away as you approach, shoot it right between the eyes. Then leave it there."'

'Why?' I felt as if someone had slapped my face.

'Because it was a more humane thing to do than to leave them to die of hunger.' Anthon paused, then looked straight at me, his eyes begging me to understand: 'The starving springbok came to the water troughs to drink. Once their bellies were full of water and they lay down under the trees to rest, they were too weak to get up again. They'd slowly starve to death right there, *Mein Schatz.* It was horrible to see.'

'But why did he send you, a mere kid?' My mind refused to understand.

'I suppose he was also a softie,' he tried to justify his father. 'By that time he'd already had to shoot more animals than he could count. And I was an excellent shot. He knew I'd be able to kill them outright. That I wouldn't prolong their suffering.'

A shadow stole through Henry. I needed to change the subject.

'I didn't realise you shoot? So you're a hunter as well?' I asked, forcing my words to appear light.

'No, I seldom hunt. If I do, it'll be for the pot. When my friend Albie tells me he's got to cull the Gemsbok on his farm, as they bred too fast and were overgrazing the veldt, I'll go out and shoot one for its meat. He doesn't enjoy shooting them either.'

'But that was it,' he continued. 'That was the moment when I knew for certain I never wanted to be a farmer.'

We drove in silence for a minute or two; the monotonous Mopane veldt still disappearing into all directions. We'd only seen one other vehicle since the last famous bend in the road.

'After this massive detour, shall we get back to Eirup?' Anthon has this wonderful ability to blow away the clouds and allow the sun back in at the flick of a hat.

'By all means. Tell me about the farm itself,' I replied.

'My family owned one of the largest farms in Namibia.

Eighty-eight thousand hectares. Can you visualise how huge that is?' A tinge of nostalgia crept into his voice.

'Let me think. How many square kilometres?' I asked.

'Eight hundred and eighty.'

Attempting to picture such an enormous piece of land proved futile.

'The farm was magnificent,' he continued.

'In my grandfather's time, our family was one the wealthiest German families in the old South West Africa. A formidable gentleman, *Opa* Richard Schröder still dressed for dinner.'

He chuckled to himself.

'Want me to paint you the picture of life at Eirup?'

'Of course! Let me see it!' I replied.

'As a small boy, I used to sit down for breakfast, all by myself, at the huge antique dining table which my great-grandfather had shipped to Lüderitzbucht; all the way from Germany. *Papa* and *Opa* had left at dawn, as dedicated farmers should. My mother was still in her room, in the process of getting herself presentable for the day, as the Lady-of-the-Manor should,' he grinned. 'My grandmother Trude was sitting on her throne, — the couch in the lounge —, knitting. Thinking up new ways to insult the next unfortunate sod to enter her domain. As the Absolute Monarch of Eirup should,' he chuckled, satisfied with his own facetiousness.

'The table was always impeccably laid. White damask table cloths, my great-grandmother Marie's Meissen porcelain from Germany, my great-grandfather's silver with the family crest on the handle, also from Germany. In the middle of the table was a tiny silver bell. I had to tinkle it only once for the cook to come and ask me whether I was ready to eat.

Dressed in a crisp white chef's uniform, she brought me my porridge with milk and sugar. Once I'd eaten that, I received a plate of eggs and bacon. Finally, she asked me whether I wanted a glass of orange juice or a cup of tea. I know it sounds extremely colonial, but it was a dignified way of living. My *Opa* Richard greatly valued respectability and good manners.'

'Nothing wrong with that,' I remarked.

'Of course,' Anthon continued, 'there was another, much less romantic side to growing up on a farm, far from civilisation.'

'And that was?' I asked.

'I was sent off to boarding school at the age of five.' I noticed how his grip tightened around the steering wheel.

'I'll never forget my first school day. My grandmother drove me to Stampriet and dropped me at the school gate. At lunch time, classes for the day were done. I went and sat in the road in front of the gate. After some time one of the older girls came to me and asked me why I was sitting there. "I'm waiting for my parents to fetch me," I answered, with great self-assurance. "Anthon, they're not coming to fetch you, you're at school now. You must sleep in the hostel tonight," she tried to explain to me kindly. "No," I told her, "you don't understand. I've been to school already. Now they must fetch me and take me back home again." She had no idea how to persuade me, so she left me there, thinking I'd come inside in my own time.'

'But I didn't give up. *'n Boer maak 'n plan,* even a German farmer could make a plan. I knew *Oom* Jan at the Post Office across the road. I also knew he was in charge of the area's farm telephone exchange. So I walked over to the Post Office. "Oom Jan," I said to him, "my name is Anthon. I live on Eirup. My parents forgot me at school. Will you please phone them and ask them to come and fetch me? I'll wait at the school gate."'

'I can't remember what his answer was. I only remember sitting outside a bit longer. Perhaps he phoned the hostel, perhaps the girl who spoke to me earlier went to tell the teacher I thought I'd be going home that evening. What I do remember is my teacher coming out into the street, holding her hand towards me. "Come with me, my boy," she said, her voice gentle. "I'll show you where you'll sleep tonight."'

'She took me into a huge room with rows of beds. Next to each bed was a cupboard. She stopped at one of them, letting go of my hand. "This is your bed, Anthon," she told me, kneeling down to my level so she could look straight into my eyes, "and this is your cupboard." I opened the wardrobe door, and there were all my clothes. My mother must've brought my stuff while I was at school. Everything was neatly packed on the shelves.'

'Nobody explained to you you'd be staying there until the weekend?' I was horrified.

'Nope. And it wasn't as if I would've had to stay until the weekend, it was for the entire term,' he replied.

'But Stampriet is hardly twenty kilometres from Eirup?' I felt anger welling up through my body. 'They were wealthy people. They had how many freakin' vehicles on the farm.' The picture of today's parents ferrying their children to and from school flashed through my mind. 'Surely they could've fetched you home every weekend at least?'

'*Mein Schatz,* I can't answer you. Most of the German farmers sent their kids to German boarding schools. Perhaps my grandparents persuaded my parents it was best to raise their kids the hard way. I've never tried to understand. But I've refused to ever do the same to my own children.'

'Still don't get it,' was all I could say, a fleeting image of my own carefree childhood in Stellenbosch surfacing from my memory.

'I remained in the school in Stampriet for six months,' he continued, 'then my parents moved me to the *Private Schule Karibib*.'

'Like in Karibib, halfway to Swakopmund?' I was hoping he'd say it was the name of a school in Mariental.

'The very same. It took my parents six hours to drive us to school at the beginning of term. In those days the roads were still mostly gravel. From then on, I only returned to the farm four times a year; for the school holidays.'

A telltale tightness gripped my throat. I couldn't fathom how an entire generation justified sending such young children to boarding school, so far from home, all in the name of 'Good Education'.

I stared out of the window, the endless white road still disappearing into nothingness far ahead, swallowed by the monotony of the encroaching Mopane veldt.

Henry lowered his song as Anthon geared him down before turning off to Opuwo.

Chapter 7

BLESSED BY THE NUNS

'Your *Opa* Richard seems to have been a remarkable man, from what I've heard from your aunt. Is he the one on that studio photograph I found?' I recently unearthed a couple of old photographs from boxes filled with discarded bric-a-brac from Eirup. All the leftovers nobody else wanted. Amongst the photographs, I found one of a distinguished looking gentleman in a three-piece suit, bow tie around his neck, the chain of a silver pocket watch visible beneath the jacket. He appeared to be in his early sixties, his full head of silver hair combed back, not a strand out of place. The family resemblance between him and Anthon was unmistakable.

'Yep. Richard Schröder. Remarkable, yes, but also remarkably hard,' he replied.

'Is he the one who first established the farm?' I asked.

'Oh no, Eirup was founded by my great-grandfather.'

'Richard's father?'

Anthon laughed. 'No, his *Schwiegervater.* What do you call that in English? His wife's father?'

'Ah! His father-in-law. So Eirup wasn't his farm, it was his wife's farm. I think I'm starting to get the picture.' I nodded my head knowingly.

So far I haven't spoken to anyone who had a kind word left for *Oma* Gertrude Schröder. According to most, she was an exceptionally nasty person. Tall and powerful, extremely plain, with no apparent need to make herself even slightly more attractive or feminine, she was hard as a rock and rude to the point of being offensive. The complete opposite of my own experience of the concept grandmother.

'Did I ever tell you about my visits to *Oma* Trude when I was a student in Stellenbosch?' Anthon asked, the Joker in charge again.

'Not that I can remember?' I answered.

'By that time *Opa* Richard was deceased, and she lived all by herself in their enormous house in Somerset West,' he began the story.

'The house designed by the Bauhaus architect Pius Pahl?' I interrupted.

'The same one, situated on the slopes of the Helderberg Mountain overlooking False Bay.'

'I studied on a student loan. Like most students, I rarely had cash to spare. Feeling it my duty, as grandson, to visit my lonely old grandmother every now and again,' his voice thick with sarcasm, 'I'd phone her to hear if I could come round for a cup of coffee. It cost me a bit to do that, as I had to pay for my own petrol. It was quite a distance from my place in Stellenbosch to where she lived.'

'She drank her coffee black but she knew I preferred mine with milk. "Stop at the corner café and buy the smallest bottle of milk you can find,'" she'd instruct me when I phoned her, "and a Cape Argus. And don't forget to bring me the slip." In those days it cost, say, four Rand and eighty cents. She'd give me a five Rand note and then demand the twenty cents change. Stingy old bitch!' he snorted.

I laughed. I was definitely getting the picture.

'Yes, Eirup was very much *Oma* Trude's inheritance,' he continued, 'but if Hitler hadn't messed up Europe, the Second World War never happened and the Russians hadn't taken East Germany, *Opa* Richard would've inherited a farm of his own.'

'Slower, you're going to fast for me. Let's start at a logical point. When did your first German forefathers arrive in Namibia?' I was getting seriously confused.

'My great-grandfather, Hans Hörlein, came from Germany to Namibia,' he complied. 'Namibia was then called *Deutsch-Südwestafrika*, or German South West Africa. It must've been in the early 1900s. A qualified engineer, he came here to take up the position of the first General Manager of the *Deutsche Diamant Gesellschaft*, which was the German Diamond Company, in Kolmanskuppe.'

'The Ghost Town? Near Lüderitzbucht? Where many of the houses have been swallowed by desert sand?'

'Yes, now known as the Ghost Town, but then still a thriving settlement related to the nearby diamond mine. Have you seen pictures of the old German house often photographed as typical of Kolmanskuppe? The one standing some distance apart from the rest of the town, towards the main Aus to Lüderitzbucht Road?' he asked.

'I've seen pictures of it, but when we visited Lüderitzbucht the wind was blowing so much we gave Kolmanskuppe a skip. I'd love to go there sometime, though. It's a photographer's dream,' I replied.

'That was where *Urgroßvater* Hans and *Urgroßmutter* Marie first lived. He started his new job shortly after they were married in Germany. I calculated it must've been just after the turn of the century. I've got an old German patient, who knew my great-grandparents from those days. According to her, Marie was always the epitome of a lady. Cultured, well-bred, yet extremely kind-hearted and generous, she was the opposite of her daughter Trude. They travelled to Europe at least once a year, both for business and leisure. After their return, the Lüderitzbucht society women waited expectantly for Marie to wear all the new dresses she brought back from Germany, then the height of fashion in Europe. Thereafter the local dressmakers had to work nonstop to copy her dresses for the local ladies.'

'Okay!' I suddenly realised something. 'That explains all the old Baedeker travel guides I found in another one of the Eirup boxes.' I filled an entire shelf with these old books, all from the era before the First World War. The pages were yellowed and brittle, whispering of another, gentler, way of life; their margins filled with notes made in Marie's fine, elegant handwriting. The Hörleins still travelled with huge trunks, fitted with drawers and hidden compartments for jewellery or cuff links, their interiors entirely covered with velvet. These travel trunks were designed to stand on one end and fold open into a wardrobe.

This particular Eirup box also yielded an ivory coloured envelope, filled with tiny dance cards. These were given to her by all her would-be dance partners at the *Silvesterball*, or New Year's Eve party, which took place on the evening of 31 December 1899. That must've been before she betrothed herself to Hans. I remember sitting with this treasure trove in my hands, on a sweltering afternoon in December. Anthon and I moved into the house in Von Eckenbrecher Street, our first joint abode in Windhoek, scarcely two weeks earlier. He was the doctor on call over the Christmas period, all four children were with their other parents and Windhoek was unbearably hot and dusty. Clouds accumulated by midday, like overdue pregnant sheep, to dissipate by sunset, leaving us sweating and gasping for a cool reprieve. All alone in this old house, still full of unknown ghosts, I attempted to create a semblance of order in our new life together. Stumbling upon this dusty box of Eirup memorabilia was like opening a tiny hole to another universe and observing someone else's life from a different time zone. The small folded dance cards had a floral picture on the one side and a name and specific dance scribbled in a nervous script on the inside. A delicate silk ribbon enabled the young would-be dance partner to tie the card around her wrist; to show she was taken, for that dance at least. I sat there looking at the date and wondered whether they had the same trepidations about the approaching century as we had about the New Millennium in 1999; whether she wondered, on that New Year's Eve, what the Twentieth Century would bring, how it would change her future. For Marie, it would bring marriage to Hans Hörlein, and a new life in the far south-western extremity of Africa. She would never return permanently to her *Heimat* in Germany. But of course, she knew nothing of this when she danced the night away.

'Marie Hörlein may have been a society lady, but she did a lot for those less fortunate than herself,' Anthon continued. 'The well known Namibian-German painter, Axel Eriksson, also lived in Lüderitzbucht. He'd fallen on hard times, drank far too much and didn't always have enough to eat. Twice a week she sent down her daughter, my grandma Trude, to take him a meal in a ménage-pot. You know, one of those pots which stack one on top op the other? The meat would be at the bottom, the vegetables in the one just above it and the rice right at the top, and then the whole lot clipped together to form a handle to carry it with. Once or twice a year, as thanks, Axel would send back one or two neatly rolled-up canvasses with Trude. Marie had them framed and hung them in her house. She had no idea they might be worth a lot of money one day.'

I was so engrossed in the lives of Anthon's forefathers, I hardly noticed that for some time the road was no longer white, but had changed to red. The flat landscape had started to undulate.

'Time for a pitstop.' Anthon brought Henry to a standstill under a large Mopane tree. I located the Stanley and our mugs and joined him in the shade, glad for a chance to stretch my legs.

'So where did the farm come in?' I needed to know more. 'Kolmanskuppe is a long way from Stampriet and the Kalahari.'

Anthon lit a cigarette while I poured each of us a cup of coffee.

'During the First World War, a well-known diamond company took over the *Deutsche Diamant Gesellschaft*. According to family legend, on entering Lüderitzbucht as the new 'protectors', the British looted German homes willy-nilly under the pretext of them now belonging to the 'enemy'. All is fair in Love and War, as the English saying goes. The house of my great-grandfather didn't escape this ill-disguised stealing and all their monographed silver and imported German porcelain were 'redistributed'. Yet the new owners retained Hans Hörlein in his position as general manager. At the end of the war, he had to attend a company board meeting in Johannesburg. After the meeting, the board members were treated to a banquet. To his shock, the entire table was laid with his own family silver and porcelain, which had been looted in Lüderitzbucht. He resigned his position the next day, demanding his property back. As grounds for his resignation, he said he couldn't work for a company which buys war loot.'

'Quite a story,' I agreed.

Anthon took the chance to take a few sips of coffee.

'This also marked the beginning of the farm story,' he continued. 'By now Hans Hörlein was a wealthy and well-respected man. He bought a farm near Stampriet, just east of Mariental, and called it Eirup. To this day you'll find Eirup marked on most Namibian maps, although it's a privately owned farm and not a village.'

'Why? What was so important about it?' I asked.

'Eirup served as the post office for the bigger farming community. The post arrived there from Windhoek once a week and was then sorted into the neighbours' postboxes.

When the farmers were in the vicinity, they collected it from us. It was also an excuse to have a beer with the neighbours, perhaps discuss the latest news and get some gossiping done.'

'He started with only one farm. A couple of years later he was able to buy a number of neighbouring farms as well. When *Opa* Richard took over, the farm comprised the entire 88,000 hectares I told you about, stocked by Hans with karakul sheep and cattle. On Eirup, the original farm, he created a real desert oasis. He built the homestead where there was abundant artesian water. By blasting holes in the *kalksteen* with dynamite, and filling them with richer soil, he planted a forest of trees around the house. When I was a little boy, those trees had grown into mature giants, towering over the farmhouse complex, creating a sanctuary of shade against the hot Kalahari Desert.'

I recalled a photograph of the dwelling, also retrieved from the now famous Eirup box. An impressive structure, the entrance had been accentuated by a massive tower which housed the water tank. Flanking this feature on either side were steeply pitched roofs cascading into the signature colonial wraparound porch. These verandahs were one of the more appropriate architectural responses to the heat adopted in Southern Africa.

By now both our cups were empty, but the half-smoked cigarette was still balanced between his fingers. I could lengthen our sojourn in the shade of the large old tree.

'So you grew up in the hot Kalahari desert?' I chucked out a new piece of bait, wondering which story I'd catch this time.

'Hot? *Mein Schatz,* today is mild in comparison.' He

leaned his elbows on Henry's bonnet, in no hurry to get back behind the steering wheel.

'My mother told me the temperature was 47 degrees Celsius in the shade on the February day when I was born. I was her second child. In those days there were no antenatal classes. *Oma* Trude was a miserable mother-in-law. My mother's own mother lived thousands of kilometres from Eirup, in the Eastern Cape, in South Africa. You didn't call your mom on the phone, over such a distance, to get birth advice. My mother was therefore totally unprepared for the possibility that my birth might proceed a lot faster than my sister's. By the time her water broke, my dad still had to drive the 83km of gravel road from the farm to the hospital in Mariental. Once she was admitted, they had to get hold of the doctor. There were no cellphones to call him while you were driving. He lived some distance from town. As he jumped out of his car in front of the hospital, the nuns screamed from the maternity ward: "Doc, make haste! You'll have to climb through the window or miss the birth!"'

'And that's why you still survive quite happily in the desert at 47 degrees?'

'Exactly.'

Anthon opened Henry's door to dispose the butt into his beer bottle ashtray. 'Guess we'd better get going.'

As we pulled away I noticed a grin on his face.

'What's so funny?' I asked.

'I suppose that's where my special relationship with the nuns comes from,' he answered.

'What do you mean? You're not Catholic?'

'That's why the relationship is so special. I think it started when I was born in that little Catholic Hospital in Mariental. I was blessed by the nuns at birth, you know.

Whilst still a baby, whenever my parents had to go to Windhoek or anywhere else, they dropped me off with those wonderful women at the convent.'

'Both you and your older sister, I suppose?' I asked.

'No, I stayed with them by myself. My sister stayed with *Oma* Trude. She didn't enjoy looking after babies. Come to think of it, the only one of her grandchildren she ever really liked was my older sister.'

'I loved staying with the nuns. They thoroughly spoilt me. Not in a bad way; we played games, they read stories to me, they allowed me to keep myself busy. For many years, photographs of me decorated the baby room of that hospital.'

'And, did being blessed by the nuns ever make a difference in your life?' I joked.

'There are those who say I was born with a golden spoon in my mouth,' he returned the quip. 'But in all seriousness, I can say yes.'

'An example?' I was sceptical.

'Since I returned to Windhoek and opened my own GP practice, I always had a wonderful relationship with the nuns at the Windhoek Roman Catholic Hospital, which I still regard as the best hospital in Namibia.'

We rounded a bend. The topography rolled away, ending in a series of low slung hills where sunlight bounced off minute patches of silver. I assumed it must be Opuwo.

'Did you not stay with your Afrikaans *Ouma* for quite a while as well?' I asked.

'Yes, I did. When I was about two and a half years old, my parents visited the family in Germany. They were away for three months. Of course I couldn't stay with the nuns that long and Oma Trude didn't see her way open to look after me, so my mom sent me to her parents in the Eastern Cape. On Eirup we spoke only German, but as my nanny also spoke Damara to me, I could speak fluent Damara as well. My other grandparents were Afrikaans. When I returned to Eirup three months later, I spoke Afrikaans to everybody, which apparently irritated old Trude greatly,' he laughed.

'So that's why you pick up accents so easily.' I've been amazed at his ability to speak three languages like a native.

I dug into the Engel for a snack. It was quite a time since we had anything to eat. I came up with a couple of apples.

'Don't worry, we'll grab a bite in Opuwo soon,' Anthon said, biting into his apple.

'I suppose I still haven't told you how the Schröders fit into the story or where they came from.'

'You're right,' I agreed. 'A fairly crucial detail, I'd say.'

'Hans and Marie Hörlein had two children. A son, Dietrich, who died of some or other liver illness when he was only ten years old, and *Oma* Trude.'

'So his name is Dietrich,' I interrupted again. 'The boy on the photo in the oval frame.' Another souvenir found in one of the Eirup boxes. A studio portrait of the young boy, dressed in a sailor shirt, so fashionable as children's clothing in the early part of the twentieth century. He looks straight at the camera with serious dark eyes, his stance strangely posed. We created a family gallery on one of the walls of our old farm-style stoep, our main summer living area in Von Eckenbrecher Street. Dietrich's photo now forms part of this display.

'My *Opa* Richard Schröder grew up on a *Landgut*, called Lischow, about ten kilometres from the town of Wismar in Mecklenburg-Vorpommern in Germany. As the eldest living son, he was destined to take over the estate one day. In preparation, he attended the University of Göttingen to study Agriculture. After graduation, he did the fashionable thing and signed up for practical experience of animal husbandry on a farm in the 'colonies'. One of Hans Hörlein's neighbours took in a group of youngsters from Germany, amongst them, my grandfather Richard. Hans invited all the young men for dinner, Richard met Trude and voilá, the match was made.'

'Ha! Hans was probably scared to death that Trude wouldn't get a husband and he and Marie would be stuck with her forever,' I laughed. 'But tell me, if Trude was as obnoxious as everybody makes her out to be, how on earth did she manage to catch a man as dashing as Richard Schröder?' I've heard many accounts of his exceptional good looks from people who were close to him. Dignified, always dressed impeccably, I was told half the women who met him were in love with him.

Anthon released a bellow of laughter before answering: 'My Afrikaans Oupa would've said, *"lus is niemand se speel-maat nie."'* — Roughly translated it means lust is nobody's playmate. —

I broke into laughter as well.

'You know, *Mein Schatz*, I've wondered whether Hans perhaps made a deal with Richard,' Anthon continued. 'He must've regarded Richard as a worthy man to take over Eirup, his prized possession. Richard was well bred, had a European education, a degree in Agriculture and his family was at that stage still wealthy landowners in Germany. Trude was Hans's only child. Maybe they made an agreement: should Richard marry Trude, he would inherit the farm. Hans could've done worse on the son-in-law front.'

'As for Richard, the prize was to be Lord and Master of one of the biggest and most successful farms in the old South West Africa,' I completed the hypothesis.

'Whichever way, they were married, my father Hans Richard was born, four years later World War Two broke out and the rest is history. In 1945 Lischow was taken by the Russians, the family fled with hardly a change of underwear and Richard no longer had a farm to inherit in Germany.'

'I suppose this last bit was a good example of putting things in a nutshell,' I laughed.

'Well, we'll have to leave the aftermath for another day. You've just reached the metropolis of Opuwo.'

Chapter 8

QUEEN ELIZABETH OF OPUWO

Entering Opuwo, the gravel road abruptly changed to tar. A bit bumpy and potholed, but asphalt nonetheless. Here we had to fill Henry's tanks with diesel for the long road ahead of us. The next possible filling station would only be at Sesfontein, at least a day's drive further on our planned route. Not that we would've had to fill there anyway. A full tank could take us one thousand two hundred kilometres, yet it was important to know where your next fuel might come from, in case of an emergency.

'*Opuwo* is a Herero word meaning finished,' Anthon explained to me. 'I find the name appropriate. In German we've got a saying, *Am Arsch der Welt;* the end, the backside of the world. I reckon, if Opuwo isn't right at the end of the world, you can certainly see it from here!'

The landscape now seemed gentle with its light green cover of seasonal grass, yet I remembered my previous trip to Opuwo only too well; dusty, dirty, dilapidated. The incongruity of the place struck me, as before: Bare-breasted Himba women strolled down the dusty streets, their postures upright and dignified, sculptured suede skirts swaying in time with their unhurried gait. Their skins glowed with a rich Indian-red, the result of a mixture of ochre and fat applied all over their bodies on a daily basis. Their hair was fashioned into intricate braids and coiffures. Handsome, wide-eyed babies strapped to their mothers' backs regarded the world with detached wonder, cradled in the safety of their earth-red leather papooses. In stark contrast, Herero women stood out in their old-fashioned Victorian-looking dresses. A style taken over from the early German settlers more than a century ago. Voluminous puffed sleeved creations of brightly coloured fabrics, sweeping down to the ground, one couldn't imagine something further removed from the simple ochre garments worn by the Himba women. The Herero women's heads were adorned with enormous ornamental headdresses of a fabric matching the dress; folded and twisted on either side to resemble the horns of a Nguni cow. Bright pinks, yellows, reds, all the colours of the rainbow in their purest hues, the scene resembled an old fashioned sepia photograph, in places hand coloured by a child with blotches of primaries.

'How do they survive wearing these long layered dresses in this scorching climate?' I wondered out loud.

'The missionaries started the fashion in an effort to make these women dress more 'properly', in the western sense. The poor sods came here from a cold Europe without their wives. They were doubtlessly so sex-starved they believed all these half-dressed wraiths were sent by the devil to tempt them. Meanwhile, their clothing reflected the climate and the available materials.' Anthon's lack of sympathy for the often misguided pious intentions of the clergy echoed my own.

'The fashion somehow evolved into a tradition denoting the marital status of a woman. Once married, she was obliged to wear the traditional dress.'

'To what extent is this custom still respected?' I asked. As a free-thinking western woman, I had difficulty imagining some of the young Herero girls of my acquaintance swapping their jeans for these ponderous costumes.

'One of my patients told me she compromises by wearing it only on national holidays or to formal functions. But the unlucky ones mightn't be given the choice by their parents and in-laws.'

'So that explains the 'traditional dress' mentioned as an alternative to 'formal dress' on diplomatic and government invitations.' I've often wondered about the quirky addition to the standard formal invite, wondering whether I should invest in a Voortrekker dress, God forbid.

'Opuwo always reminds me of a scene in one of the old Star Wars movies. The scene which comes to mind is the one where an array of the main characters enter a town and nonchalantly intermingles with a hotchpotch of the most amazing creatures,' I commented. 'I wouldn't blink an eye if Princess Leila or Darth Vader had to walk down this street right now, with all these Himba and Herero men and women, the youngsters dressed in Cool, the poor people in rags. That guy must be a local businessman. Look at his black suit!'

The man in question was dressed in a black, tight-fitting three-piece suit, cerise pink shirt, purple tie and shiny, sharply pointed black and white patent leather shoes. Standing with feet apart, hands folded behind his back, perspiration pearled on his closely shaven head. He surveyed his home turf with the supremacy entitled only to One-Eye in the land of the blind.

'Makes sense,' Anthon nodded.

'What does?' I asked.

'Read the sign above the door behind him.'

'Lucky Woodwork,' I read, 'Coffins for Life.' Underneath the slogan, a crude sketch of a coffin completed the picture.

I burst out laughing. Our sharp-looking gentleman in black was most likely the local undertaker.

We crawled patiently behind a donkey cart. Driven by an old man in a neat jacket and vintage felt hat, his customers were two enormous Herero ladies in full traditional regalia, each holding a brightly coloured umbrella for protection against the searing sun. A couple of boys on outmoded big-rimmed bicycles overtook us, swerving not to hit the various species of livestock crossing the street whenever a particular piece of edible rubbish on the opposite side appeared more enticing.

We passed a tyre repair shop. Consisting of a corrugated iron shack, open towards the street, a huge variety of new and second-hand tyres were displayed outside on the pavement. A man, presumably the salesman, or perhaps the repairman, was draped languidly over the length of the display, cap pulled over his head, for all we knew, fast asleep.

A convoy of five rental 4x4 vehicles was parked next to the road. All four were white. All were fitted with rooftop tents and roof racks. Each had a blue gas canister fitted into a round bracket behind the tent. And all screamed the name of a car rental agency from every conceivable surface. The occupants were standing next to their vehicles. Dressed in khaki, exactly alike, as if their outfits were standard issue rented with the vehicle. Using hands, feet, and every other means at their disposal, they were attempting to negotiate with a group of Himba women carrying large baskets of beads and bracelets. As we edged past, our windows wide open, we overheard one of the men trying to explain what he was looking for to one of the Himba girls. She clearly didn't understand English. He seemed to believe if he shouted slowly with articulated syllables, accompanied by expressive arm and hand gestures while staring directly into the innocent Other-Language-Speaker's eyes, it might magically translate into Herero, the language the Himba speaks. It sounded something like this: 'I,' (extended vowel with lots of banging on his breast with his hands), 'waaaaant,' (arms flying in wide circles for no other reason than not being able to think of another gesture for 'want') 'HUN-TING,' (this word very loud as it was very important, accompanied by the pose of a hunter shooting a rifle), 'Knife!' (here he gave a relieved smile and made a chopping movement with his hand, looking more like a nifty karate move than anything else). The poor Himba woman reversed backwards with each word he uttered, while he kept on advancing until I expected her to turn around and run away in a cloud of dust.

We both laughed until we had tears in our eyes.

'I don't understand this Out-of-Africa, Safari Look compulsion of so many tourists travelling in Namibia,' I ranted once I got my breath back. 'Surely they don't dress that way back home, wherever that may be? Why advertise your status as a tourist so blatantly?'

'Perhaps they think us Africans all dress like this,' Anthon speculated. 'Or otherwise, they might wish to camouflage themselves from the wild animals roaming freely everywhere!' Anthon burst out laughing. We were always amazed at some of the naive perceptions abounding about Africa amongst visitors from the 'developed' world.

'We joke about international travellers expecting elephant and lion in the streets of Windhoek, whilst assuming they'll come down with malaria, yellow fever or a host of other tropical diseases the minute they get off the plane at Hosea Kutako Airport. First world doctors make loads of money with useless, inappropriate inoculations requested by uninformed tourists,' he added.

We pulled in at the filling station. I noticed a group of Himba women sitting in the shade of a large tree, baskets piled high with copper bracelets and necklaces.

'I'm going to take a look at what they've got to sell, while you fill Henry.' Hanging my camera around my neck, I squeezed out of the door. Little urchins with outstretched hands were already clamouring to be the first to beg for sweets or money.

A corpulent *meme*, dressed in western clothing, sat in the centre of the group. She was surrounded by traditionally adorned women and children. The unmistakable spokesperson, I asked her whether she spoke Afrikaans or English. Beaming, she answered me in the well-modulated Afrikaans often encountered in Namibia. Offering her hand in greeting, she introduced herself.

'I am Queen Elizabeth of Opuwo,' she said with a wide smile. Taking my outstretched hand in hers, we performed the traditional African handshake, consisting of a series of grips with changing thumb positions. The greeting over, she waved her arm in a wide sweeping movement, indicating all the various wares exhibited in handwoven baskets in front of her: 'I've got lovely Himba jewellery to sell.'

I wanted to buy copper bracelets for the girls, but have been searching for some time for one of the rarer authentic Himba shell necklaces, which were fast becoming collector's pieces. I'm addicted to beautiful things, especially if handcrafted. Kelims, silk sumacs, hand blown glass, amber or carved wooden beads; I love them all. I have one important rule, though: where possible, I want to buy it at the source where it was crafted.

But first I had to negotiate a price for taking a few photographs of the women and children. Many tourists don't understand why they have to pay to take photographs of these people, yet the Himba keep their attire so immaculate precisely because it provides them with an income. It's a joy to photograph them. Proud of their appearance, they love to pose for photos. After each shot they wanted to see the digital image on the back of my camera, commenting vociferously in Herero.

Anthon joined us. He delighted in conversing with Queen Elizabeth in a mixture of Afrikaans and Herero. By now she realised we weren't tourists and not interested in the curio shop trinkets. Her attitude changed. She called one of the younger boys and gave him instructions in Herero. Disappearing into the crowd, he shortly returned with a couple of the necklaces I was after, but not of the best quality. Authentic Himba adornments were exclusively made from natural materials, like leather, beads, horn and shells. Most of the newer pieces, manufactured specifically with the tourist-trade in mind, incorporate pieces of rubber or plastic, especially as a base for the beads and shells.

'My *meme* wants one of your real necklaces,' Anthon explained to her. 'One like that one, over there, the one with the large shell.'

Anthon pointed to a necklace worn by an attractive Himba girl. An enormous sea shell hung between her bare breasts; ivory white with tiny, regularly spaced brown markings marching as if in regiment around the curving cone. The shell, hanging with its narrow apex pointing downwards, was suspended on a couple of leather cords, strung with closely packed rough metal beads. A T-section incorporating a few brass beads held the mollusc in place. The curve and colour of the shell were in striking contrast to the fine textured, earthy red of her skin. Above this necklace, a multitude of decorative wire, metal and leather pieces twirled and twisted exuberantly around her neck. If I couldn't buy the piece, I surely intended to take a few photographs of it.

Queen Elizabeth turned her head towards the object of our attention, then nodded in understanding. She rubbed her chin, her eyes focused on an idea stirring deep inside her mind. All her sales abilities were now functioning in top gear. Those necklaces were expensive. She could earn a good commission with such a deal.

'No, no, no. That one is not for sale.' She turned her gaze back to us. 'That shell was collected by the *meme's* grandmother herself at the Kunene River Mouth, a long, long time ago. They walked for many days to find it.' She paused to give us time to appreciate how arduous the journey was. 'She gave it to her daughter, and her daughter gave it to her daughter, who's that *meme*.' She pointed at the girl in question.

By now the girl had become aware of our attention and moved closer, enabling us to get a detailed view of the exquisite piece.

Queen Elizabeth spoke to her in Herero. She dropped her gaze, shaking her head from side to side, then she spoke at length in Herero, gesticulating with her hands and pointing to a chubby baby sitting on the ground.

'No, no, she can't sell this one to you. When her daughter is old enough the shell will be passed on to her.'

I must admit, I doubt whether I'd feel comfortable buying a genuine heirloom from one of these proud Himba women, merely to hang on my verandah wall at home. It's fitting that it should be passed on through the generations. I just didn't want one with plastic or rubber replacing the original leather.

Queen Elizabeth narrowed her eyes, her forehead furrowing in concentration. She had a plan. 'Hmmm,' she scratched her chin again, staring into the crowd, 'maybe I can get hold of one.'

'How long will it take?' Anthon was eager to continue our journey. The sun was moving towards its zenith.

She shook her head, clearly figuring out how best to handle this sale. 'Not today.'

She paused for a moment. 'Not tomorrow.'

'When are you coming back to Opuwo?' We told her earlier that we regularly drive up to Ruacana.

'In about a month's time,' he replied, 'but how will we get hold of you?' He didn't believe he'd ever be able to find her amongst this throng of people again. Queen Elizabeth's face lit up.

'You just ask anybody around here for Queen Elizabeth of Opuwo. Everybody in Opuwo knows me.' She thrust her hand into her ample bosom, searching for something.

'And I can also give you my number,' she delightedly produced a cell phone from its safe hiding place inside her bra. She waved to a small boy playing in the dust not far from us. 'Come and read my number, Eliphas,' she said to him. 'I've got an important order from this *meme*. She must know where to phone me when she comes back.'

That's all part of the incongruity of this town. An African lady, called Queen Elizabeth of Opuwo, with a modern mobile phone hidden away in her bosom, the hindrance of illiteracy solved by one of her literate children.

We did go back, one month later. Anthon phoned Queen Elizabeth on the day before we planned to pass through Opuwo. They agreed on a time. Same place. When we arrived, she was sitting in the exact same spot, under her tree, like a queen bee surrounded by her subordinates. On recognising us, she took out a plastic bag hidden under the wide folds of her dress and spread a breathtaking collection of handcrafted pieces in front of us. We walked away with a treasure trove of authentic Himba adornments, although I insisted to be reassured I wouldn't be party to cheating a little girl out of her rightful inheritance. Queen Elizabeth smiled all the way to the bank. As she most probably planned, we bought much more than just a necklace.

Chapter 9

THE MAN WHO WANTED TO SHAKE THE DOCTOR'S HAND

The hinterland from here to the Skeleton Coast is inhospitable and barren. Temperatures often rise into the high forties during the heat of the day, only to drop to below freezing at night. We had to be on our way. I still had no idea where Anthon intended camping for the night.

'One more essential to buy.' Disappearing into Opuwo's

only supermarket, he soon returned with two bags of ice which he packed into the Engel.

'Nothing as decadent as having sundowners, with a few cubes of ice, when you sit miles from nowhere in the middle of the African desert.' The details often make all the difference.

As we left town, the tarred road turned into dusty red. Settlements became sparser and soon all signs of human habitation were left behind.

'Before I met you, I used to come to Opuwo at least once a month.' He gave a dry chuckle, as if he was looking at another self from a great distance and found the image somewhat comical.

'To do what?' I made no effort to hide my astonishment. The vision of filth and dust was still too fresh in my memory. 'Surely not because you wanted to?' I couldn't help adding.

He laughed, this time from deep inside. 'As a matter of fact, I even looked forward to it.'

I looked at him obliquely. I wasn't sure whether it was meant ironically.

'Well, I came to Opuwo every four to five weeks to run a clinic for the local people,' he confessed.

'Isn't there a state hospital here?' I was rather surprised. I had to do feasibility studies for at least three new primary health care clinics in this region many years ago. At the time a small state medical facility was being constructed in the town.

'There is, but the nurses only hand out contraceptives and treat malaria and tuberculosis. Lately, they also do AIDS awareness and antiretroviral treatment. All other conditions are treated with a handful of paracetamol tablets and a couple of coloured vitamin capsules.' His tone was resigned. 'There's such a need for doctors out here. Do you know how many people have to struggle through life with diseases which are easily curable with affordable western medicines?'

'Such as?'

'Something as common as a bladder infection,' he answered. 'Imagine you're one of these local women who've got to work in the fields under the hot sun every day. You suffer from a chronic bladder infection. The clinic gives you painkillers and vitamins.'

I cringed at the thought. There are few conditions as uncomfortable as a bladder infection, as most women would know.

'So you're a philanthropist as well?'

'Perhaps,' he turned to face me, grinning like an imp, 'but it also gave me an excellent excuse to get away from the missus.'

I just shook my head and smiled.

'Why Opuwo? I find it to be one of the most miserable places I've ever visited.'

'I suppose circumstances dumped me there. When I first started doing clinics for Nampower in Ruacana, I drove from Windhoek to Ruacana in one day, attended to the clinic early the next morning and finished at lunchtime, too late to return to Windhoek. I prefer not to drive after dark: too big a chance of hitting a donkey or a kudu.'

'Is it really that dangerous to drive at night?' I digressed, 'I can understand the danger of a donkey on the road, but why are there so many fatal accidents involving kudu rather than other types of game?'

'They often graze in the road reserve,' Anthon explained.

'If you've seen a kudu hop over a two-metre high fence with no effort at all, you'll understand how natural it is for them to leap over obstacles. For some reason their reflex reaction to the oncoming headlights of a car is to jump into the road, attempting to jump over the danger rather than to run away from it. If a fully grown bull, weighing all but two hundred kilograms, crashes through your windscreen while you're driving between 80 to 120km per hour, your chances of survival are slim.'

'Okay, I get why you would rather drive during day time. But how did that bring you to out-of-the-way Opuwo?' I asked.

'Give me a chance, I'm getting there!' Anthon laughed. 'You're the one who asked about the kudus.'

He settled more comfortably into his seat, scratched around for his cigarettes and shook another one out of the packet.

'One of the headmen from the Kunene Region heard about my monthly trips to Ruacana,' he steadied Henry's steering wheel between his elbows, enabling him to light the match with his one hand while shielding it with the other. It was too hot to even consider winding up the window merely to light a cigarette.

'He made an appointment at my surgery in Windhoek to come and see me.'

I decided to make myself comfortable as well and slid down a bit further in my seat, resting my left foot on Henry's dashboard, right against the door.

'Dressed in a suit and tie, he seated himself across from me in my consulting room. At first, he didn't say a word. His body language told me he was on official business. He had something important to ask me. I asked how I could help him. "Doctor," he answered, "I didn't come here today because I'm sick. I came here, from Opuwo, to ask you to come and help my people, because many of them need a good doctor." He looked at me with a grave expression. I was a bit taken aback, especially as I also knew about the recently completed health facility. "But what about your new hospital?" I asked him. "Surely there must be medical personnel available to see your people?"'

'"Doctor," he answered, "we don't want the medicine they give at the clinic. It's not good. We want real medicine. We're prepared to pay for that medicine if it'll help cure our illnesses. There's no private doctor in Opuwo we can go to. There's no private pharmacy we can buy our medicine from."'

'I told him I'd think about it and let him know. Why not? I asked myself. It would be a refreshing change from seeing snot noses and gippo-guts all day.' He chuckled, flicking a column of ash out of the open window. 'I adapted my schedule to leave Ruacana at lunchtime, drive to Opuwo and examine patients until dark, spend the night in town and leave for Windhoek early the next morning. Before my next trip up north, I phoned the headman and told him I'd come, but had no idea where I'd be able to examine the patients. He was delighted. "Just come, doctor, we'll provide you with a place to see the people," he promised.'

'Didn't you have to cart an awful lot of equipment with you to do the examinations?' I asked.

'Not really,' Anthon replied. 'I always have my stethoscope, E&T set and blood pressure monitor with me anyway. For the rest, I needed my hands, my eyes, my experience and my brain.'

'What about medicines?' I persisted. 'You mentioned there being no pharmacy either?'

'I had a fair idea of what medical problems I might find. I ordered a variety of medications and packed them in a cool box. The first visit was a fairly short one. I first needed to see how it would go and whether there would really be any interest. The headman did his job well. There were more patients than I could see in the available time. My clinic became a regular event and was soon extended to two days.'

'As the word spread, the local radio station broadcasted the dates of my visits well in advance. Sick people came from miles around the town and waited patiently for a day or more to be examined by the doctor.'

'You still haven't told me where you conducted these examinations?' I interrupted again.

'The headman provided me with a mud hut with a tin roof and no windows,' Anthon chuckled. 'At times the temperature inside soared into the mid-forties. Yet I loved it. It gave me the most amazing satisfaction to treat these people.' He turned towards me again. '*Mein Schatz,* do you know how good it feels when you know you were able to improve someone's quality of life? Some of these people struggled with really debilitating conditions for years; illnesses which could easily be cured, with the correct diagnosis and treatment.'

I looked out of the window. Rugged hills flanked the road on either side. Cumulus clouds bulged against the sky in the distance.

'I know what you're talking about.' I replied.

'You do?'

'Not the medical treatment bit,' I laughed, 'but I was also involved in work which bettered people's lives.'

'Care to elaborate?' he prodded.

'Some of my work here in Namibia involved rural development projects, like clinics and school hostels,' I explained. 'The first clinic site handover I conducted in the Omusati Region was an eye-opener for me. I assumed the meeting would be a formality, and imagined it would proceed as follows: Show the contractor the drawings and the locality, read the standard list of do's and don'ts, then hang around at the Ondangwa airport in the heat for the rest of the day, waiting for the plane to return to Windhoek.'

'To my surprise, when we arrived at the site, the entire community, from the headman and the Clinic Committee to the Parish Priest were sitting in the shade of a large Sausage Tree, chairs and benches hauled from the nearby school to seat us all. Dressed in their Sunday best, each dignitary made a speech thanking us for the wonderful deed we were doing for their community. The headman couldn't speak English, so the nurse patiently translated every sentence for us. After the speeches they sang and danced, ending the proceedings with a long prayer, again thanking God for sending us to their humble village. For the construction team it was just another smallish government job which had to be completed, but for this community, a life-changing event. Once the clinic was built, they'd no longer have to walk twenty kilometres through the countryside for treatment when they were ill. I found the experience pretty humbling. It made me aware, once again, of how much easier my life was than the lives of those villagers.'

From Henry's window, I watched as a handful of Himba huts glided past; tiny red ochre beehives scattered some distance apart on a barren clearing of whitish clay. I wondered where they collected their water, where their nearest clinic was.

Anthon pressed my hand, sharing the emotion without words. I poured us a cup of coffee. We drove in silence while I concentrated on keeping the coffee inside the cup as Henry swayed over the undulating track.

'In these out-of-the-way rural areas few people can speak English,' Anthon picked up where we left off a few kilometres earlier. 'For my clinics in Opuwo, I employed a translator to help me communicate with the Ovahimba. My Herero keeps me out of trouble, but is far from fluent enough to allow me to take a patient's case history and make a diagnosis.'

'Any special stories?' I nudged.

'Many,' he chuckled, 'but I've got a favourite.'

'So?' I urged as he just sat there, arms wrapped around Henry's steering wheel, smiling at his own recollection.

'One morning an Ovahimba man came to see me. I asked the translator to find out what his ailment was. The man explained he'd been suffering from diarrhoea for many years. His life was miserable. He had little energy and was desperate for a cure. He'd been to the State Hospital on numerous occasions where he always had to sit in line for the entire day, just to be sent home with a little yellow plastic envelope filled with paracetamol tablets and a few multivitamins.'

Anthon navigated Henry through a slippery puddle. The carved Makalani seeds dangling from the rear-view mirror swung rhythmically from side to side.

'I listened to his story, then prompted the translator to get him to list all his symptoms. His was a classic case of Amoebiasis, an illness often contracted by people drinking water from communal wells, which were also used by animals. Although it's a horrible disease it's quite easy to cure with the correct treatment.'

'As I told you before, I always took a variety of medicines along to Opuwo. I gave him the right medication to effectively cure his condition and explained how he should take it. He paid me for the consultation, couldn't thank me enough and went on his way.'

We drove through another patch of mud. Blobs of clay plonked onto the windscreen, shuddered, then wriggled sideways, painting brown squiggles across my field of vision.

'Two months later, on one of my subsequent visits to Opuwo, I saw the same man sitting amongst the waiting patients. While busy with the queue of people in front of him, I racked my brain, trying to figure out how I could possibly have misdiagnosed him before. He merely sat there, showing no sign of being impatient or agitated, waiting for his turn to talk to me. When I came to him, I asked the translator to find out why the *tate kuru* was back, whether the medication didn't improve his condition.'

'Explain to me what exactly *tate kuru* means,' I interjected, 'you've been using the word often.'

'A *tate* is a man and *kuru* translates as old. Not old in the negative, western sense, but rather as a form of respect. Calling a man a *tate kuru* is therefore a respectful way to address a male person of your own age or older. For a woman, you would use *meme,* as I called you just now when we spoke to Queen Elizabeth.'

'Okay. Now it makes sense,' I said. 'So what did the translator say?'

'He told me, "No, Doctor, he says he's never been better.

He came back to shake your hand and to tell you that you're a blessed man; that you changed his life; that God will bless you for what you did for him." You could've pushed me over with your little finger, the answer was so unexpected. I asked the interpreter to find out where the man lived, curious to know how far he'd travelled to see me. "Doctor," he answered, after a lengthy consultation with the old man, which included a lot of arm swinging and pointing into the distance, "If you walk from here, 90km into the mountains, that way," he pointed in a north-westerly direction, "you'd get to the village where he lives."

'Do you know what the most amazing part about treating these people is?' Anthon continued, 'After the consultation, they'd take out a roll of banknotes and pay you in cash. I often took brand name medicines as well as their cheaper generic counterparts to Opuwo. I'd put both in front of the *tate kuru,* explaining the difference. He'd take time to think, first picking up the one, then the other, weighing his options. In most cases, he'd decide to take the more expensive trademark medication.'

'Working in these rural parts does teach one humility,' I said. 'We're so quick to criticise and judge. People often assume a rural existence without a western-style education necessarily makes you a lesser human being. Yet, who's the greater person? This Ovahimba man, living a dignified tribal life, in total harmony with his environment in the far-off mountains in Kaokoveld? Or the city slicker, living in his modern house surrounded by a lush garden in an expensive Windhoek suburb, yet complaining about his existential angst to his therapist during his costly weekly sessions?'

'Nobody is right or wrong, *Mein Schatz,*' he replied, his voice gentle, 'we all have to deal with different problems and different circumstances. I like to believe we all have different lessons. Do you not always tell me it depends on one's viewpoint? One of my disabled patients, who's confined to a wheelchair, confronted me with this truth one day. He said to me, "Doc Anthon, we all have our wheelchairs. Everybody can see mine, but no one can see yours."'

'My forefathers were staunch Calvinists,' I said, 'all sincerely believing they were ordained to make the lives of these people better by teaching them to read, then providing them with Bibles and a new set of rules. Calvinist rules, mostly. Yet, more often than not, they interfered with a system developed over centuries, with a balance as much part of nature as the ecosystem in a natural pond.'

'You're so right,' Anthon replied. 'Now you know why Opuwo is such a desolate place. In contrast, the remote Ovahimba villages are alive; the traditional lifestyle balanced by the laws inherent in such a community.'

'The missionaries not only brought Bibles, but they also judged a moral code which regulated society effectively. Their zeal to replace it with a totally foreign ethical concept destroyed the fabric holding the delicate system in place. Alcohol, which ironically came with the traders who followed the evangelists, did the rest.' I added.

'And proved much more popular and life-changing to the entire social structure than the missionaries' message,' Anthon concluded.

Chapter 10

KAOKO-OTAVI, WHERE YOU PAY YOUR GUIDE WITH A BALLPOINT PEN

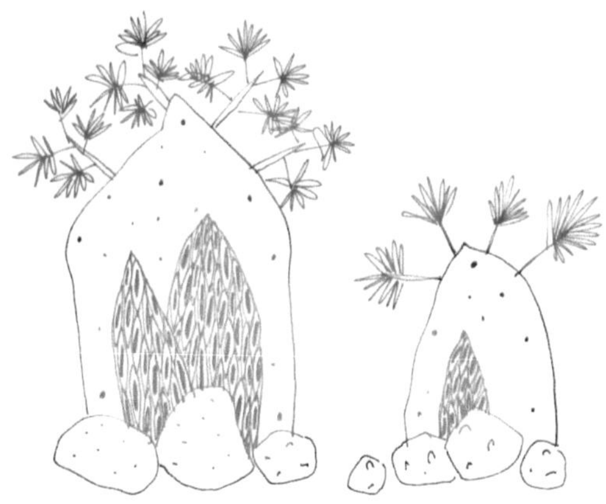

After leaving Opuwo the red of the road had become more intense, still clammy with the previous night's rain. The rural track hugged the contours of the countryside, crawling up and down hills which undulated like swells on a storm-pregnant sea. Every rise anticipated an abrupt descent to a V-shaped hollow, transformed into a potential wheel puncturing gully by the seasonal rain. Gigantic Boababs guarded the foot of a *koppie,* — as we call a small hill in Afrikaans —, entirely consisting of a pile of massive boulders. We passed a T-junction. The signpost pointing in the direction we were going loudly proclaimed Ka ko t vi, half the characters obliterated by red mud.

'Kaoko-Otavi,' Anthon filled in the missing letters. 'Ever heard of the place?'

'Heard of the place? I've been there,' I said triumphantly.

'But you told me you've never camped north-west of Korixas in your previous life?' He sounded surprised.

'The trip had nothing to do with camping and relaxation. All work related. Quite eventful as well, come to think of it,' I recalled.

'Sounds interesting. Are you going to tell me about it?' he niggled.

'Let me think. Where to start?' I tried to grab hold of a thread which might lead me to the appropriate place to begin. We still had so much to catch up on.

'Well, here goes. Remember the story I told you about the stone for that project in Oshakati?'

'The one you did with Pete?'

'That one, yes. Did I mention the firm I worked for?'

'Not that I can recall right now. Refresh my memory?'

'A year after we came to Namibia, I was appointed as a senior architect with B & Partners.'

'Mr B's firm? No, you never mentioned you worked for him. I know him well,' Anthon interjected.

'Then you'll not be surprised if I regard him as a bit of a male chauvinist?'

He chuckled before he gave a cautious reply: 'He likes to project the image of a liberal, progressive gentleman.'

'Perhaps that's his official public persona,' I continued. 'In the office, he derived much pleasure from pushing any girl, who dared compete on male turf, to her limit. Naively, I often fell for it. I took on tasks my male colleagues shuddered to do just to prove I was as capable as they were. Struggling with my own ego issues at the time, I suppose. I needed to prove my female superiority at all cost.' It suddenly struck me I used to be as sexist as Mr B.

'My first project consisted of conducting those feasibility studies, which I mentioned earlier, for new primary health care clinics in the Kaokoveld. Never having done a government feasibility study before, I had no idea how the system worked. The public sector, as your client, differs in so many ways from working for the private sector.'

'First explain to me what you mean by 'feasibility study',' Anthon interjected.

'In the construction industry, a feasibility study is an investigation into the need for and logistics surrounding a proposed project. It's then presented as a document compiling all information, including the potential cost, for future budgeting and planning.'

'Sounds involved,' Anthon nodded.

'It is,' I continued. 'The process includes an inspection to view the site, assess the terrain, the vegetation, establish how to reach it, — often the road leading to the village proved to be a mere track —, availability of services like water or electricity, disposal of sewerage and so on. We also have to consult the regional representative of the relevant ministry to discuss their needs and prepare drawings detailed enough for an accurate cost estimate.'

'So you've got to travel to the area before the feasibility can be finalised?' he asked.

'Of course! And that's where this story starts. Back in 1999, fresh in Namibia from Cape Town, I regarded the Kaokoveld as a far off place one travelled to after months of serious planning. Not ten years before, it was still a war zone. I had no idea what to expect. Mr B gave me a basic briefing before instructing me to get on with it. I tried to locate the sites for these clinics on a map, but couldn't find a single one. He sent me off to the offices of the Surveyor General to obtain detailed maps; enormous sheets covered with tiny annotations and hundreds of contours and levels. On these I had to track down place names unfamiliar to my ear, Oruvandjai, Otjiu, Ohandungu. Many of the place names were similar, except for one letter, like Epoko and Epako, and every tiny village was named.'

'After I wasted a day with this effort, one of the more experienced architects suggested simply phoning the Ministry of Health's regional office in Opuwo and asking them for directions. I was so green I didn't even realise the ministry had a regional office in Opuwo. I was ready to shoot my boss.'

'Sounds like the Mr B I know.' Anthon chuckled.

Telling the story so many years later, I had to smile at the girl I saw in my mind's eye. Back then my sense of humour wasn't always present. Life was a Serious Business. As I continued with my recollection, I realised the person I was talking about was as fictitious to me as it must've been to Anthon. I continued with interest, wondering what else my former self might reveal.

'When I finally obtained the right telephone number and managed to get hold of a knowledgable person, they told me to just come to Opuwo. They'd take me to the various sites in a government vehicle.'

'Oh my God!' Anthon groaned, 'Did Mr B explain to you what you could expect? I can just imagine you sitting in the front of a bombed-out *bakkie*, squeezed between the health official and three relatives who needed to take their goats, all on the back of the vehicle of course, to the village you just happened to be going to. Did he not tell you how many years he worked in the North when he was younger? He knew the area like the back of his hand.'

I laughed. 'I told you he did it on purpose. He gave me zero advice. I admit I was more stubborn than most in my youth, but he really pushed my boundaries. I assumed he expected me to refuse, which would've confirmed his well-voiced theory regarding the superiority of the male species, and justified why he paid me less than the guys on my level.'

'Did you ever consider he might've respected your abilities more than you realised at the time?' Anthon suggested.

'Perhaps,' I conceded, 'but he could've offered more advice regarding the planning of the trip, especially as the intricacies increased: of the seven hundred kilometres between Opuwo and Windhoek, more than half consisted of rural gravel roads. One needed an off-road vehicle, which I didn't possess. The airstrip at Opuwo was in a poor condition and the commercial pilots preferred not to use it. Chartering a plane for one person was in any event not cost effective. The only other possibility was flying to Ondangwa with Air Namibia, renting a vehicle and then driving to Opuwo.'

'We used to call our famous National Airline *Scare Namibia.*' Anthon interjected mischievously. 'Even so,

Opuwo is still about two hundred and seventy kilometres west of Ondangwa.'

'Don't run ahead of my story, I warned you it was going to be a long one,' I laughed.

'Okay, I'll shut up; but I'm starting to feel sorry for you, *Mein Schatz.*'

'Logic wins hands down when ego is involved, my dear,' I went on. 'I explained my plan to Mr B. He approved it without adding any further guidance from his side.'

'Don't tell me you intended undertaking this trip by yourself?' Anthon knew about my aversion to driving on gravel.

'I like to regard myself as a Strong Woman, however, I'm not that tough.' We both laughed.

'No, on my insistence the Boss allowed one of the guys in the office to accompany me. He chose a twenty-something called Jaco, a youngster who started at B & Partners only a month earlier. This guy was an architectural technician and one of those awkward macho Afrikaner-types who carried a heavy chip on his shoulder. Not having had the grades to go to Archi School and get the qualification, he believed he knew more about architecture than most architects. Females didn't feature on his scale of worthy construction professionals. To crown it all, he'd never been north of Windhoek or driven a 4x4 on gravel in his life, — this I, unfortunately, found out much later —, yet he oozed enough testosterone to consider himself capable of entering the Dakar-to-Paris rally.'

I took a sip from my water bottle as the temperature was now close to 39 degrees Celsius and rising. We relied on open windows to provide some form of evaporative cooling.

'Well, to continue my long story, I bought a copy of the

latest Shell map of Namibia, in the late nineties the best source of information available to novices on the roads in the Kaokoveld. Remember, this took place before affordable GPS's and Google Earth. In truth, Mr B didn't allow internet in the office, as he believed we'd all be spending company hours surfing the net for porn.'

'Ha!' Anthon chuckled. 'People always accuse others of what they do, or want to do themselves.'

'Except poor old Mr B didn't even know how to switch on a computer,' I laughed. 'He once sat next to one of the guys discussing a project. He accidentally touched the button on the keyboard which activated the screen saver. Remember the one which simulated an exploding universe? Mr B nearly had a heart attack. He thought he'd crashed the machine. We ragged him about that for years afterwards.' I chuckled at the recollection. I must admit, I've since softened my opinion of Mr B, but at the time he sure knew how to get my back up.

'This map showed a road leading straight from Ondangwa to Opuwo,' I continued.

'Oh no! Are you serious? The only route runs north through Ruacana and then south-west in the direction of Kamanjab.' Anthon interjected again. 'To this day a straight road from Ondangwa to Opuwo doesn't exist. Too many *Oshanas* in the way.'

The topography of Northern Namibia, which is commonly referred to as Ovamboland, is flat to the extreme and stretches into Angola. During the rainy season, the volume of rain falling in the more tropical southern Angola causes a massive flood, known as the *Efundja,* which gradually seeps into northern Namibia's Cuvelai Basin, filling every hollow and indentation in the flat landscape with water. These shallow ponds and lakes are called *Oshanas* in Oshiwambo.

'How was Jaco or I to know that? Without trustworthy advice from anybody in the office, I blundered on. I booked our plane tickets, based on the assumption we'd be able to fly from Windhoek on the 6am flight, arrive in Ondangwa at 8am, pick up the car and reach Opuwo by lunchtime. Judging from my Surveyor General map, I calculated we might even have time for the first site visit the same afternoon.'

By now Anthon was roaring with laughter next to me, but I was on a roll.

'In those days, Opuwo had only one lodge. I therefore made reservations for two nights, thinking one full day should allow us plenty of time to get to the other sites, and scheduled our return flights to Windhoek for the next afternoon.'

Revisiting this absolute folly, the hilarity of it hit home. I burst out laughing as well.

'As you can imagine, we landed in Ondangwa and picked up the sole 4x4 vehicle available for rent in the region. —Incidentally, ten years later we still use Cheetah Car Rentals, but now he owns an entire fleet of off-road SUV's.— Jaco revelled in his role as the driver of this piece of macho machinery and we left Ondangwa in good spirits. We only bought a couple of Cokes for the road, planning to have lunch in Opuwo.'

Anthon groaned at the utter stupidity of the whole exercise.

'Within half an hour we might've been driving in Saskatchewan. The map proved completely useless. Typical of rural Ovamboland, the gravel road shortly dissolved into two sandy tracks, which again forked into a myriad of smaller possibilities, animal trails and footpaths. Furthermore, the landscape is flat and featureless. We soon found ourselves in the middle of a *mahango* field watched over by an old man. His behaviour made it clear he was the owner of the land and we were the trespassers. Unable to communicate in any other language than Oshiwambo, he gesticulated with his knob *kierie* to emphasise whatever he screamed at us. Clearly translating into 'Get the fuck out of my crop or ...!' Jaco changed into reverse gear, leaving deep furrows in the soil as we retreated as fast as our vehicle would allow us. Two hours later we arrived in a small village, where we were directed to a woman who could speak a few words of Afrikaans. She laughed at us and pointed to another track. Using the sun as our point of reference, we attempted to continue due west, hoping to reach the road between Kamanjab and Ruacana and on to Opuwo.'

'It was November. Some call it suicide month, due to the mercilessness of the dry heat. Thankfully the rainy season hadn't started, as we would've been stuck in an *Oshana* within the first hour. By this time our Cokes were empty and our stomachs hollow, yet what could we do but keep going?'

'I gather somehow you did survive, as you eventually even made it to Kaoko-Otavi?' Anthon niggled.

'Well, it was pointless to try and turn back, as we had no idea where back was. After hours of sandy tracks, small villages and helpful villagers, we stumbled upon the long white road to Ruacana we've just driven on. We arrived at Ohakane Lodge as the day drew to an end. Sweaty, dusty, hungry, tired, appalled by the utter desolation of the Regional Town of Opuwo.'

'I stayed at the same place when I did my clinics. Imagine us having been there simultaneously?' Anthon said. 'How many other places could our paths not have crossed in?'

'Can you recall how dry it was in 1999?' I continued. 'We drove into Opuwo as the setting sun lit up the dust particles in the air. I then realised the romantic photographs often displayed in National Geographic, of African people and cattle walking into the dusty splendour of sunset, frequently hid a stark reality of poverty and refuse and human misery. The villages we passed through in Ovamboland were orderly and clean, the inhabitants had dignity. Arriving in Opuwo, I was overwhelmed by the despair of the place. The Ovahimba I encountered away from Opuwo were stately and dignified. The hordes I saw on that day were the dregs of society, the drunks, the beggars, the outcasts. Coming from Windhoek, then known for its cleanliness, the rubbish littering the streets hit me between the eyes.'

'To think I conducted my clinics there once a month,' Anthon reflected.

'Did your family have any idea under what circumstances you worked?' I asked.

'I tried to share the experience with the ex, but she showed little interest. She didn't mind how I earned her living, as long as I handed it over immediately,' he exploded with mirth at his own cleverness. 'So what happened next?'

'Although a tiny, basic lodge, I've never been so grateful to have my own room, with a bathroom and hot water,' I continued. 'Not to mention the evening meal, taken under the *lapa*, the cool night air resuscitating my travel weary body. The lodge owner just laughed and shook her head upon hearing how we struggled to find the 'road' from

Ondangwa to Opuwo. She told us to go back via Ruacana. Even though appearing much longer on the map, the first part, up to Ruacana, was good quality gravel. The rest was tarred to Ondangwa. All of which I know now, of course.'

'Anyway, the next morning we met with the official from the regional office of the Ministry of Health, Mr Innocence Haipinge.'

'"We *aal*-a bit ... how *sharr* I say ... *undel*-equipped at the moment," he regretted to inform us, wringing his hands, looking everywhere but into our eyes. "We've got to take you to Otjiu in the *am-bu-rance,* but we've got *onry* the one..." he shook his head from side to side, while ruefully shaking his hand, one finger pointing heavenwards, "...so if *de'rs* an *e-me-gency* ..." He paused to allow the possible consequence of such a grave occurrence to hang heavily between us. Still having difficulty with the switched r's and l's, as well as the heavy rural accent, I struggled to comprehend what he was trying to say. "I think he wants us to go in the ambulance," Jaco whispered to me under his breath. Horrified at the thought, I immediately suggested using our rented 4 x 4, as long as he accompanied us to show us the way. By the width of his smile, he must secretly have had this in mind from the start.'

'Can I guess what happened next?' Anthon chipped in. 'He collected a couple of friends or family members who just happened to be in need of a lift to the same place you were going to.'

'How did you know?' I regretted the question even before I voiced it out loud, deserving his increasing merriment. Mortified, I put my foot even deeper into it: 'We also asked the lodge to pack us some lunch and cool drinks for the day, but didn't contend with our government official who believed it to be our duty, as previously and currently advantaged people, to provide for him, as a previously disadvantaged person.'

'You were so extremely green,' Anthon laughed.

'But he was a government employee on a good salary with benefits,' I tried to justify myself, but it only made him laugh more.

'We then set out for the first clinic, Otjiu,' I decided to ignore him.

'There's a place called Otjiu shown on our map,' Anthon remembered. 'We'll pass through it later this afternoon.'

'Same place. The previous day I was a bit concerned about Jaco's driving speed, but it was nothing compared to this trip. The road between Opuwo and Kaoko-Otavi, this road, was a proper gravel road. Jaco's testosterone level was sky high. He pushed the vehicle to 120km an hour on the flat stretches. Our passengers grumbled amongst themselves in the back seat, but Jaco was in rally mode and ignored all comments or advice. Every time we descended into one of these depressions between the hills, he stepped hard on the brakes causing the car to bounce through the dip. Once I heard how Innocence bumped his head against the roof of the car. Later it sounded like our passengers were praying in Herero. I tactfully started a discussion around the increase in accidents involving tourists rolling their rented vehicles on gravel roads, but Jaco didn't get the hint. Not to sound like the nagging female, I kept my mouth shut, like a fool.'

'This road?' Anthon's voice sounded incredulous. 'He drove 120 on this road?'

'Yep,' I confirmed.

'Was he mad? Even driving at 70km per hour would've been dangerous.'

'And this brings me to the Kaoko Otavi part.'

'Just in time. The village lies straight ahead.' Anthon pointed at a clump of gigantic wild fig trees in the distance.

'Right here Jaco still raced at more than 120km per hour. The terrified Innocence tried to alert him to some sort of imminent danger. He kept blabbering about the '*virrage*' and a '*livir*' ahead, but Jaco was deaf to any advice not originating from his testicles.'

'Look out!' I exclaimed as Henry bumped through a sharp indentation. Anthon skilfully navigated a narrow but deep stone culvert, built diagonally across the road, clear water rushing along its length.

'The exact culvert Innocence must've been ranting about,' Anthon commented. 'One comes upon it so suddenly there's little time to react. We just crossed it at 60km per hour and the jolt was forceful. It brings water from a natural spring to the village.'

'Well,' I continued, 'Jaco came tearing over the hill before he spotted the village. Too late, the imbecile stepped on the brakes, our vehicle skidded on the gravel, hit the culvert and veered sharply to the left. The ground on my side of the car approached at a frightening pace. I expected us to roll. Miraculously the momentum wasn't enough, as the road inclines to the opposite direction, so the car righted itself as we came to a halt. I emerged from the car with jelly legs, but otherwise unscathed. Innocence had to pacify a whole gaggle of angry villagers, conglomerating as if from nowhere around us. I had the urge to attack Jaco myself, even more so after spotting the two flat tyres on my side of the car. Thankfully the car came with two spares. I was too furious to offer any assistance with the changing of the tyres. Neither did Innocence or the villagers care to help.'

'I don't blame them. He could've killed someone. These villagers are normally friendly and helpful,' Anthon said.

'After listening to Innocence blowing off steam about Jaco's recklessness and how they hardly ever drove at more than 40km per hour on this road, I calmed myself by taking photographs of the houses.'

At that moment we passed through the village. Neat clay houses lined the ochre road. Two small windows flanked each central entrance, the door just high enough for a man of average height to pass through. Walls, textured by half-moon patterns created by hands rubbing wet clay onto wattle and daub, slanted at whimsical angles. It resembled a child's drawing of a village. Here and there discarded hub caps, which most likely popped loose from vehicles driving through the ditch too fast, were built into the walls for ventilation, adding to the quirkiness of the buildings. Fencing wires sagged between gnarled Mopane fence poles, casting abstract patterns on the uneven surfaces of the clay structures. A massive wild fig towered over a number of houses, sheltering the tiny dwellings in the depths of its cool shade.

'What a gigantic tree! It must be at least forty metres in diameter,' I exclaimed.

'I think half the village will fit under it.' Anthon agreed. 'Shall we see if we can find the ruins of the church?'

'There was a church here?' I asked, rather surprised.

'This is quite a historical spot,' Anthon answered. 'How much do you know about the *Dorsland Trek*?'

'Not a great deal, I must admit.'

'To my knowledge,' he proceeded to explain, 'the Dorsland Trekkers were an offshoot of the Great Trek, which took place when disgruntled farmers wanted to move away from the British government in the Cape and find a place to govern themselves. They'd hardly formed the Boer Republics when gold was found in the Transvaal. The Brits couldn't resist the temptation to extend their powers yet again. A number of Boers, now seriously pissed off, packed their wagons and set off for the promised milk and honey of Southern Angola. They took a tortuous road through the former Bechuanaland and into Northern Namibia, from where they crossed the Kunene River into Angola at Swartbooisdrift. In Angola, the milk turned sour and the honey bitter when the Portuguese Government proved to be no different from the British, resulting in yet another packing of wagons and yet another trek back to South Africa, this time via Namibia. Hardship and malaria devastated their numbers, but a handful settled in this country. Kaoko-Otavi was such a settlement.

'The signpost to the ruins,' Anthon pointed to a small marker leading us to a bumpy track. The ruins proved to be no more than the foundations of the tiny church which used to stand there. By the time we found a place to park Henry, we'd already collected three teenage boys, self-importantly vying to be our guides. They assumed we were overseas tourists, but Anthon caught them off guard by greeting them in Herero.

Impressed, their attitudes changed from insolent self-importance to complete brotherhood. They bombarded us with questions.

'Do you live in Windhoek?'

'What's it like to go to a movie?'

'My uncle lives in Katutura and he's got his own car!'

'Is it true in Windhoek the children go to school in taxis?'

'One day, when I finish school, I'm going to study at Unam!'

We answered what we could, then asked the boys how much they wanted for 'showing' us the ruins.

'*Meme*, have you got ballpoint pens?' one fourteen-year-old asked me with large serious black eyes.

I was completely taken aback. So used to these rural children begging for sweets, the request caught me off guard.

'*Meme*, we've got books, but no pens. We can't buy any in Kaoko-Otavi and Opuwo is too far. We need pens more than money.'

I wanted to cry. The ideal of education for all fails in so many seemingly insignificant ways. What use are exercise books if you've nothing to write with?

'Well, luckily Father Christmas just rode into town in a Land Rover.' Anthon had the smug expression of a satisfied feline. I was as clueless as the boys, straining their necks to see what he was doing in Henry's drawer.

'Here you are! Courtesy of all the major pharmaceutical companies in Namibia.' With the flair of a magician unveiling a golden goblet, he brought forth two hands full of colourful pens from his medical bag. I burst out laughing when I read the inscriptions on some of them, Viagra, Cialis.

'The last substance they need more of in this part of the world!' I grinned and shook my head at the contradictions confronting us around every corner.

The excitement of the boys infected us with a renewed appreciation for the abundance we enjoyed wherever we went. We gave them each a cooldrink and a few apples, as thanks for teaching us a valuable life lesson.

As we got back into Henry, I turned to Anthon, 'We've got so many people around us suffering from a chronic melancholy; always miserable with what they've got, where they are in life. Yet, everything is so relative. For these boys,

Windhoek is the unattainable Dream City and being given a couple of ballpoint pens the highlight of their week.'

'While back home, kids complain to me about depression when their parents refuse to provide them with the latest model of Cool,' Anthon completed my thought.

AT THE TIME of completing this book, nearly twenty years after my first encounter with Kaoko-Otavi, a beautiful tarred road had been built from Oshakati to Opuwo. I also look back at Mr B, who'd passed away recently, with much softer eyes. Perhaps he was wiser than my youthful self gave him credit for and realised I needed to discover for myself what my capabilities were.

Chapter 11

OTJIU, DESERT LILIES AND MAKALANI SEEDS

Back on the road to Orupembe, we passed a flat expanse where the red clay collected so much water that it had been churned into a sticky sludge by vehicles and animals. The track forked into a delta of possibilities as drivers preceding us had tried to dodge the Mopane trees. With Henry, negotiating the stretch of mud was simple, the sturdy engine steadily propelling the old vehicle forward. Once through the bad patch, Anthon returned to my story.

'So, I assume, after the accident at Kaoko Otavi, you were continuing further on this road without a single spare tyre?'

'Yep,' I answered. 'We also didn't have extra water, warm jackets or food. Knowing what I know now, I shudder at what could've happened should we've had another flat tyre.'

When Anthon and I undertake one of our trips, however hastily planned, we always make sure Henry's drinking water tank is full. We pack a saucepan and dried food like pasta for at least three extra days. We also pack warm clothing and plan where we'd be able to obtain diesel. The filling stations in the remote areas often run dry. A jerry can or two with extra fuel is therefore indispensable.

'And I can imagine you also didn't have anything like my Land Rover Recovery Plan in place,' Anthon's voice sounded nonchalant.

'Your Land Rover Recovery Plan?' I couldn't recall ever hearing about such an insurance.

'I never leave Windhoek without making sure it's activated and paid up.' He looked at me with serious grey-blue eyes.

'Where does one get such a plan?' I stepped in it again.

'Firstly, you need friends,' he launched his explanation. 'Friends who are True Believers.'

Henry's engine droned loudly.

'Sorry, I can't seem to hear you correctly. The friends must be what?' I was confused.

'True Believers,' he repeated, the frown across his forehead emphasising his words.

'True believers that Toyota is the One, the Only, the Be-all and End-all of off-road vehicles.'

'And?' I jerked my head sideways to face him squarely, suspicion rising as fast as my blush as I realised he'd caught me with my foot in it again.

He stretched out his left arm and ruffled my hair while exploding with laughter.

'It's a real plan, *Mein Schatz*, you can ask any of my friends. That is, any of my Toyota Driver friends. I always phone one or two of them before I leave Windhoek. For this trip, JP is my Recoverer. I told him exactly what route I intended taking and roughly when I should be where. If he doesn't hear from me within a few hours of the times we'd agreed upon, he'll come and search for us.'

'That's the plan?' I was a bit disappointed. I expected something much more dramatic, at least involving a helicopter or something. 'And why would your friends be so eager to drop everything and drive out to the Kaokoveld just because you didn't phone exactly when you said you would?'

'It's all based in human psychology. To a Toyota driver, the idea of towing a Land Rover into Windhoek is irresistible.'

Repressing a smile, I shook my head. 'Perhaps I should be more tolerant of a particular brand of male testosterone.'

Then I had an afterthought: 'But you lied to catch me. You said the plan must be paid up.'

'Of course it must be paid up. Your friends must believe you're an equally devout Land Rover Driver. Otherwise, you might not return the service when they happen to be the ones getting stuck in the wilderness. Do you realise just how proud it would make me to be the one to tow a Land Cruiser into Windhoek?' He cracked another deep hearty laugh.

'And while we're on the subject, let me share a well-kept secret about Toyota Land Cruisers with you. Do you know why they write '4,500' on its side?'

'It's probably the engine size?' I tried.

He said nothing, just looked at me.

'No?' I asked. I thought for once I had an intelligent answer about a car.

'It's the only 4x4 in the world which indicates on its side how many meters it can drive with a litre of fuel.'

This time I was the one to do the slapping, and not of the steering wheel; though I must admit, I thoroughly enjoyed laughing with him.

We were now driving through the enormous flood plain formed by one of the tributaries of the Hoarisib, east of Otjiu. The rainy season had been good. The normally powder-white earth was covered with silvery-green grass, swaying in the breeze; hiding the harsh desert underneath a soft veneer of foliage.

'When I first set eyes on this plain, the day of my rather unpleasant Kaoko-Otavi experience, the endless expanse of chalky dust overwhelmed me,' I said. 'The incredulous thing was, there were a number of apple-green arrow-like lilies growing straight out of this barrenness without a single leaf surrounding their stems. Not in a cluster, but one here, then one over there, ten meters further. The effect was surreal.'

I was still talking when Anthon whooped with excitement, 'Look at that enormous field of flowers!'

All I could make out was an infinite expanse of grassland and a large area of what appeared to be white desert sand. My distant vision was becoming too blurred for my liking.

'Over there! Don't you see it?' He brought Henry to a standstill and rushed out, leaving the engine idling and the door wide open.

I strained my eyes to improve my focus. The patch of white transformed into thousands upon thousands of snowy Nerine lilies, blooming in this remote desert valley, for no-one's pleasure but their own.

'Consider the lilies of the fields, they neither labour nor spin,' the words tumbled from my mouth by themselves, but Anthon was already on his haunches in the midst of a dense stand of flowers. I strolled towards him with my camera. A sudden urge to prostrate myself amongst such grandeur, forced me down on my knees, then flat on my stomach. Submerged in acres of blooms, I wondered whether life can be any more perfect than this moment. From my worm's-eye view, Anthon was dwarfed by the majesty of the massive river valley. Hazy blue mountains contained the vastness, shimmering in the distance. The moment was too profound for me. Here I was with the most special man I ever met, the only man I ever wanted to grow old with, and the Universe rolled out this display of magnificence.

Just for us.

For free.

Abundance comes to us in many forms. A tear smudged my camera's eyepiece.

After half an hour of delighting in this spectacle, a cup of coffee from the Stanley, and many photographs later, we continued on our journey.

Soon after, we passed a solitary Ovahimba man, with naked torso and traditional leather skirt, the longer skins at the back swaying from side to side as he walked. His feet were bare, his stick in his hand, a dog trotting behind him. A proud warrior appearing like a mirage from another dimension.

'Did we drive past a village somewhere?' I couldn't remember seeing any sign of human habitation for some time.

Anthon waved to the man, who returned his greeting. 'They're an amazing people. They'll walk through this ruthless land for enormous distances, notwithstanding the heat. They really know how to live in harmony with nature.'

Much further we passed a tiny settlement, mud and twig beehive-shaped huts perched on the dusty barren ground, fleeting and impermanent.

'The village seems to be deserted,' I commented.

'The Ovahimba people are nomadic herders,' Anthon explained. 'They move with their cattle between areas where they can find grazing and water. On leaving, they close up their huts, leaving a few utensils inside, for when they return.'

'So a deserted village doesn't mean it's been abandoned?'

'Not at all. A different group will respect the huts as belonging to someone else. When two branches are left crossed over the entrance, it implies entering will be regarded as trespassing. Travellers, such as us, should show the same consideration and not disturb their belongings.'

A couple of kilometres further a signpost with an arrow pointing into nowhere materialised out of the haze. It advertised ice cold Coca Cola, what else? The sign was as absurd in this emptiness as the thought of a shop where one could buy a bottle of chilled cooldrink.

'Let's follow the pointer.' A sudden thirst welled up in my throat.

The faint track took us towards a sprinkle of Makalani Palms, which had been beckoning us across the valley for the last twenty minutes.

I grabbed Anthon's arm. 'I've always wanted to fill a huge Owambo basket with Makalani seeds. Perhaps we'll be able to pick some up?'

He grinned.

'You're such a hoarder. But you've convinced me.'

As the palms came closer, we realised they marked a trickle of water bordering the southern fringe of the plain. The Hoarisib River, instrumental in carving this massive valley, now runs on the northern edge. I suppose the word 'run' is a misnomer. These rivers appear bone dry for most of the year, although they're frequently described as 'flowing' under the sand. A heavy summer thunderstorm, striking much further upstream, could transform a dormant watercourse into a seething deluge of murky water. The floodwater gathers all the vegetation which collected in the riverbed during the dry season and deposits it meters higher on the river bank. Or in the sturdy branches of an old Ana tree; there to dangle like absurd decorations once the torrent had subsided again.

We reached an abandoned structure constructed out of driftwood. The palm leaf roof, bleached silver-grey by the sun, cast a deep shade. Two crows perched on the erstwhile service counter. Their beaks yawned wide because of the heat. Or were they merely astounded by the sight of two humans and their Land Rover? Another tattered cooldrink advertisement splashed the black-and-white composition with a dash of red.

We parked in the shade of a large Makalani. Anthon concluded all the cooldrink propaganda had by now awakened a mighty thirst in him. He dove into the Engel and dug out an ice cold beer. Too impatient to fetch a hat from the back of the vehicle, I went in search of makalani seeds. I soon found a mass of the shiny brown nuts, a bit smaller than tennis balls, strewn under a clump of palms. Forming a cradle with the front of my T-shirt, I gathered as many as the stretched top would allow, then lugged them back to Henry.

'Have we got something to put these beauties in?' I shouted from a distance, immensely proud of my find. Anthon merely waved a bottle at me. To the crows' annoyance, he'd made himself at home in the shade of the kiosk. Stretched out on a camping chair, cigarette in one hand, he was savouring his beer. I dumped my hoard of nuts next to him, then sat down on the ground. The heat pounded in my ears; the offered bottle of juice a refreshing relief.

'You're as red as the billboard. Why didn't you put your hat on?' he scolded.

I still underestimate the sting of the Namibian sun. 'I spent no more than ten minutes out there,' I attempted an excuse.

Our thirst sated, we found an empty shopping bag for the seeds. To thank the crows for the use of their shade, I crumbled a piece of leftover sandwich under their perch. They seemed indifferent about our presence or absence.

'Have you seen the curios they carve from these Makalani nut kernels?' We were back on the road. Anthon had one of the berry brown orbs in his hand, testing the hardness of it against Henry's dashboard.

'Yes,' I replied, grabbing hold of what appeared to be a large bead covered with African wildlife, dangling at the end of a leather band fastened to Henry's rear-view mirror. 'This!' Then I added, my tone smug, 'and I've fallen for the trick the locals use to sell them to you as well.' Two boys approach you while waiting at the service station to fill your tank, or when you stop to look at some of the roadside curio stalls. The first one starts up a conversation, casually asking your name, where you're from, whether you're enjoying your trip, while the second one would stand quietly in the background, carving something. Just when you want to leave, this boy proudly presents you with a carved Makalani kernel, covered with intricately chiselled wild animals and crowned with your own name. How can anybody refuse to buy it?

'At least they're worth the couple of dollars you pay for them. It's quite a mission to get the kernel out of that hard shell, and it takes some skill to carve them so finely.'

And it makes the ideal gift to hand out to family and friends from outside Namibia.

'There's the signpost for the Otjiu Clinic,' I said as we drove past a standard Ministry of Health name board. Behind it a simple rectangular building with a large shady verandah was visible. A faded red cross painted on the white roof confirmed its status. The Namibian flag lazily stirred at the top of the regulatory flag pole, reminding us of the existence of Government within this primeval land we found ourselves in.

Apart from the Himba man we passed a while ago, we hadn't encountered another vehicle or living being since leaving Kaoko-Otavi. The clinic appeared deserted, although the presence of a few items of clothing clinging to a nearby washing line suggested at least humans were lurking somewhere out of sight; probably observing us from beneath the depths of the shady verandah.

Soon after we reached a vast riverbed. Although now a

benign dribble of water, the might of the previous flood was still visible. Massive arboreal skeletons wedged against the Ana trees standing their ground on the river banks.

'We'll have to walk this one before attempting to drive through.' Leaning with both arms on the steering wheel, Anthon peered at the riverbed, searching for the most suitable place to cross.

'Meet the Hoarisib, one of the mightiest rivers of the Kaokoveld.' I could hear the awe in his voice.

'I need to establish how deep the water is and whether the riverbed is firm enough for ol' Henry's weight. It appears to have come down recently. The sand might be too soft.'

I considered asking him what he'd do if it did turn out to be too soft, but I knew the answer. We'd have to drive along the bank and search for a better crossing. Here time didn't exist, no deadline had to be met. If darkness caught you before you reached your planned camping spot for the night, you camped where you were and continued on your journey the next day. The present moment was nowhere more accessible than right where you were.

Quite happy to take off my shoes and wade into the shallow stream, I was surprised to find the water lukewarm. The sand felt firm under my feet. I splashed my legs and arms with the clear water, allowing the wind to cool my limbs for the few seconds it took before my skin was dry again.

'We should make it.' Our joint verdict as we reached the other side of the river.

'This is a must-have photo.' I was looking back towards Henry, dwarfed by a backdrop of tall Makalani palms, the only man-made object in this immense landscape. He seemed diminutive and forlorn on the other side of the river. We walked back hand in hand, splashing each other as we kicked our feet hard into the water with each stride we took.

I collected my camera. Anthon was to wait until I was on the other bank again. As he slowly made his way towards me, I took a series of shots of the approaching Land Rover, thankful we got through without a glitch. Should you get stuck here, you might have to wait a couple of days for someone to come past and pull you out; should they happen to be driving a suitable vehicle. Or a sudden rainstorm didn't cause the river to flood first, in which case one could end up with a Landie half buried under the sand. But then again, we had Anthon's Land Rover Recovery Plan and the testosterone of his friends to rely on, I suppose.

Chapter 12

A YELLOW BUTTERFLY ON AN ELEPHANT'S FOOT

Driving out of the river valley, we travelled into a landscape in sharp contrast to the savannah we just left. Massive, barren mountains towered ahead, the road all the while climbing steeply above the Hoarisib, which now ran to the south of us. The expanse of the valley receded in the rear-view mirror. The Hoarisib veered off to the left, disappearing behind another mountain range in the distance, in its search for the Atlantic Ocean. The road had deteriorated to a track scratched out between rocks and over boulders, snaking through the inhospitable mountains like an ant trail. As if out of nowhere, a vehicle appeared, driven by a solitary Chinese man. In all likelihood a contractor building another insignificant outpost of government somewhere in the wilderness. We pulled to the side of the road to let him pass. After the dust had settled, we again had the road, the valley, the entire universe, to ourselves.

The late afternoon light was tinged with amber, subtly softening the formidable landscape. Driving due west, every tiny particle floating in the air was transformed into a shimmering speck of gold. Almost through the mountains, as we rounded a bend, we unexpectedly found ourselves amongst a herd of cattle. The majestic animals, horns as wide as a man's outstretched arms, filled the entire track and seemed to continue into infinity. They ambled towards us without haste, silent silhouettes with gilded contours.

'Nguni cattle,' Anthon observed with appreciation, the inborn instinct of a farmer's son taking over. 'Aren't they splendid!'

I regarded the variations in their hides with awe: dark brown flecked with white, white freckled with ochre-red, black speckled with white and brown. They were in perfect condition, fat and healthy.

We advanced at a snail's pace, the endless mass of bovines parting in front of Henry to let us pass. I felt as if we were floating on an ocean of hides and horns.

'They're gorgeous,' I said. 'But where do they come from? To whom do they belong? What do they graze on?' I found it surreal.

We were now at least five minutes' drive into the herd

and still the Nguni's kept on coming. Out of nowhere, a young Himba man rode up on his horse, his muscular bare torso held proud and fierce. He waved at us, gave a loud whistle and disappeared into the shimmering cloud of dust. An apparition from another world.

'The herd boy,' Anthon explained. 'He communicates with his animals by whistling. This herd must belong to one of the tribes in the area.'

'How do they feed them during the dry season?'

Anthon pulled away from the window as an enormous horn glided past within millimetres of his head.

'Nguni cattle have a remarkable ability to adapt to the harshest African environments. They're much less prone to sickness and tick infestation than their more highly bred commercial cousins.'

We entered a narrow gorge. Gearing down into first, we inched forward to allow the animals to pass us in single file.

'Their herdsmen know the desert like we know the cities we live in. As young herdboys they're taught where to find water during the dry season and when grazing should be available in which valley. They're at one with nature, always on the move with their animals.'

'Where did the Nguni originate from?'

'Iron Age nomadic people brought the first animals to South Africa. The European colonists thought they were inferior and tried to 'better' them by interbreeding them with exotic cattle. It's only as recently as the late twentieth century that agricultural researchers have bothered to study them. To their surprise, they figured out Ngunis are more suitable to Southern African conditions than any other cattle.'

It took us another ten minutes to draw clear of the herd.

'The Himbas measure their wealth by their cattle.' Anthon could safely hang his elbow out of Henry's window again.

'The tribe owning this herd must be very rich,' I stated the obvious.

'Well, think about it,'he speculated, 'they don't have a bond on a property to pay off, they don't need household insurance, car insurance, life insurance or medical insurance. They've got no municipal rates and taxes to pay.'

'And to them, a household alarm system with armed response is as foreign as space travel,' I added.

'Except for VAT, they don't pay tax,' he continued, 'for how do you tax nomads on their communal land, inherited from their ancestors? They don't have to keep up with the Jones' house, cars or clothing. When they need something they can only buy in a shop, they sell a cow and pay cash. They get milk and meat from their cattle. I sometimes think they're much wealthier than we are.'

'And that herd boy we saw just now, is as free as an eagle,' I concluded.

The track through the mountains had been rough, but the rocky descent on the other side was formidable. Anthon brought Henry to a standstill a few meters from a sharp drop into a craggy ravine.

'What do we do now?' With hesitation, I released my grip on the grab rail under the side window.

'We show you why a Land Rover is still the Best Four by Four by Far.' Anthon gripped the steering wheel with his right hand, shot me a satisfied grin and pushed the gear lever into first. Without effort the vehicle lowered itself over the rocks, crawling down the stony cliff like a giant dung beetle, gripping each rock with its sturdy tyres until we came to a standstill in a horizontal position. It felt good to open the door and feel the river sand under my bare feet, but it was getting late. I had no idea how far we still had to go. I resisted the urge to ask him whether I could have a closer look at the enticing pebbles winking at me from a distance.

'We must be close to Orupembe by now,' he noted a while later.

'All I can see is another vast expanse of emptiness. Nothing which resembles a town,' I disagreed.

'What makes you think we're looking for a town?' he chuckled. 'I expect a couple of houses, a windmill, a shop and maybe a service station.'

Not long after the zigzag carcass of a windmill appeared against the late afternoon sky. Coming closer, we noticed it was accompanied by two tiny buildings. One of them proclaimed 'Orupembe Shop Nr 1' on a bright red facade, again advertising Ice Cold Coca Cola.

'Coca Cola seems to have a hundred per cent market share in this vicinity,' was my dry comment.

Apart from the carcass of a canary yellow pickup truck, a dented water tank and a distant outhouse, a woman sitting in the shade of the hut was the only sign of human habitation in this bare landscape.

'Just as well Henry has a second diesel tank. No service station here,' Anthon said.

As Henry chugged up the hill on the other side of Orupembe, the stately shape of an oryx materialised at its crest. The profile of its remarkable horns carved in ebony against the lowering sun. I grabbed my camera and considered attempting a shot, but decided against it. As we passed, he lifted his head and stared at us, his tall shadow rolling away into the valley towards Orupembe.

'I still have no idea where we're camping tonight.' The gleaming sky reminded me that night was fast approaching.

'To tell you the truth, neither have I.' Anthon shrugged his shoulders, a mischievous twitch around his mouth.

'I've got a plan, though. I'm just not sure whether I'll find the place again.'

The landscape was now surreal. The expanse of reddish-brown earth receded towards the coast, merging with the sky in the distance. Sporadic chunks of rock, each with an elongated shadow of charcoal in its wake, created a perspective reminiscent of De Chirico. Emaciated sprigs of dried grass flamed against the horizon. The beauty was overwhelming.

'Many years ago I took the extended family on a camping trip to the Brandberg,' Anthon said, a slight smirk audible in his voice. 'We drove through a similar landscape. One of the women was horrified at the desolation. "God must've been very angry when he created this," was her only reaction. I realised her religious zeal prevented her from seeing God when he was standing naked right in front of her, like here. Why do so many people confuse God with Religion?'

There was no time to discuss this interesting hypothesis. Without warning, he gripped the steering wheel and veered sharply to the right.

'Hold on!' he shouted.

Henry vaulted over the sandy ridge forming the edge of the track, moulded by the bulldozer the last time the road was graded. After another bounce or two, he steadied the vehicle, casually continuing as if it was a perfectly normal thing to do.

'Why did you do that?' I was still clutching the seat in fright.

He shrugged, his concentration focused on the distant hills.

'I'm sorry, *Mein Schatz,* but this is the road we must take.'

The path we now followed consisted of two feint tracks hardly discernible from the surrounding rocky plain. We headed towards a cluster of *koppies*. The topography dropped into a lower-lying area, appearing to be an ancient riverbed. Here Anthon brought Henry to a standstill. While the engine was still idling, he turned to me with a satisfied grin.

'Your abode for the night, *Mein Schatz*.'

The last rays of daylight blinded our eyes, telling us to hurry. We rushed to set up our camp before dark. This time we prepared the bed with our fluffy down duvet. It can be freezing cold in the desert at night, even in the middle of summer. Half an hour later we were sitting next to a blazing campfire, each holding a gin and tonic complete with cubes of ice, courtesy of the Opuwo Supermarket. A magical display was rolling out all around us.

As the last glimmer of orange faded from view, we both fell into quiet contemplation. Tranquillity seeped into our beings, our surroundings dissolving into mauves and pinks and an incandescent indigo sky.

A loud rumble from Anthon's stomach dropped me back into the desert.

'We haven't had a decent meal since this morning. Let's start cooking!' he confirmed what his abdomen had already let slip.

Suddenly ravenous, we unpacked our dinner and laid the table for the meal. Jacket potatoes were wrapped in tinfoil and placed directly on the coals. While we waited for them to cook, I assembled a fresh green salad, dressed with a trickle of olive oil and a squeeze of our own balsamic reduction. We unpacked our wine glasses, carefully wrapped in dishcloths and stored in a special wooden box. He opened a bottle of Reserve Pinotage. Anthon was in charge of the oryx fillet, which he seared to perfection over the red-hot coals, sealing in the tender, rare meat. I unpacked the *coup de grace* from the cooler, a small container of *salsa verde,* prepared from a variety of our own home-grown herbs. The perfect accompaniment to the meat.

'To life!' Anthon lifted his glass and touched mine. A shard of sound challenged the silence of the desert. 'Can it get any better than this, *Mein Schatz*?' he sighed.

Having finished our meal, we moved closer to the fire.

'Why here?' I asked. I've wondered about it since we left the gravel road.

Suspecting a story might be attached, best told at the campfire over a glass of wine, I contained my curiosity.

'This was Ben's favourite place on earth,' he answered, his eyes soft. His gaze turned inward.

'Ben?' I couldn't remember him mentioning a 'Ben' before, but then again, he knew so many people, it would take me years to remember and place all of them.

'Ben's life touched mine only briefly. Yet he'll always be part of my story.' Anthon took a sip of his wine, gathering his thoughts.

'Touched, as if past tense?' I asked, but he continued as if he didn't hear me.

'I met Ben when I started my housemanship year. I

noticed him during the orientation session. At first, he stood out due to his height; he was at least two meters tall, with olive skin and black hair.' He twirled his glass between his thumb and middle finger.

'But something else intrigued me. When he introduced himself, he looked at me with a directness, an honesty unusual in a stranger. I saw something gentle in his eyes, but also something ancient, transcending centuries. I knew we would always be friends. I knew we had always been friends.'

Firelight flickered on his face. He was elsewhere, somewhere far away.

'We started chatting. The usual background talk. I noticed he wore a wedding ring. "My wife has been my only sweetheart since we were seventeen years old," he told me with a shy laugh. I felt a stab of envy at the time. I wished I was so lucky.'

Anthon brought the wine glass towards his lips, then suspended the movement in midair. A splash of ruby brushed his cheeks and mirrored in his eyes.

'Ben introduced his wife Lisa to me. The three of us became close friends. I felt comfortable with them. It was as if we were family. We could talk for hours, about everything. Or about nothing, if none of us felt like talking.'

He took a sip from the glass, then placed it back on the table.

'We often went camping together. On one of our trips we came up here, to Ougams fountain and the Bear Road; the route we'll follow tomorrow. One evening the three of us were sitting on one of those rocky hills in the distance, looking over the desert towards the Skeleton Coast. We were chatting, bantering as friends do. Out of the blue, Ben said:

"When I die, you must come and scatter my ashes here. On this exact spot." I burst into laughter. "Ben," I replied, "I'm older than you. We're both not yet thirty. By the time you die, I'll be unable to climb these *koppies* with my walking stick." Lisa smiled at this, but Ben didn't laugh.'

'He looked at us without his habitual lazy smile. "Promise me!" he insisted, a strange urgency in his voice. "Please?" He looked at us in turn, his eyes serious, questioning. "Promise me?" he repeated. Rattled and uncomfortable, I agreed with an "Okay, okay, I promise!" I remember feeling mildly irritated. The mood was broken.'

'By the next morning, all was forgotten. We never spoke about it again.'

He topped-up our wine. Firelight exploded into the glasses with rich velvety red.

'We didn't have much contact over the next year or two. I moved to Cape Town, three years later they moved to Canada. Ben wanted to make some money to repay his study loan. By the time we moved back to Windhoek and I'd opened my own surgery, they'd already left Namibia.'

He put another piece of wood on the fire. I waited silently for the story to continue, afraid to break the spell.

'Ben and Lisa were in Canada for about two years,' he continued. 'We had sporadic contact, mostly by mail. International phone calls were exorbitantly expensive in those days. One morning my receptionist put a call through to me. I was so surprised to hear his voice, that my first reaction was to ask him whether something was the matter.'

'"Why would there be?" he answered, "Just felt like talking to you." I told him my waiting room was sitting full of patients. I asked whether I could phone him back later. "Let them wait," he replied. "I want to talk to you now." The old Ben. I could see his whimsical smile as he said that. We ended up chatting for at least half an hour.'

He sipped some more wine, his eyes fixed on the fire.

'What did you talk about?' I asked.

'Nothing in particular. We reminisced about things we did together in Namibia, chatted about their life in Canada and the imminent arrival of their first baby.'

'A couple of days later I got a phone call from Lisa. "Ben is dead," I said when I heard her voice'

'"Yes," she answered. "You know what we'll have to do." My head was reeling. "I'll organise everything," I promised her.'

'I knew he was dead, *Mein Schatz,* I just knew. Lisa told me later that he also phoned his father, whom he hadn't seen in years.'

Anthon gazed into his wine, firelight skimming off the layer of sadness glazing his eyes.

'How did he die?' I slipped my hand into his.

'I can only give you my recollection of what I heard at the time,' he answered, his emotions under control again.

'Ben was a keen sportsman. He loved cycling. In Namibia, he used to ride through the desert for fun. All by himself. In Canada, he often cycled from one town to the other, with Lisa driving in front of him in their Kombi, as backup vehicle. That morning he went for his breakfast ride. As usual, she drove in front. Lisa told me how something prompted her to look in the rear-view mirror. Ben was right behind, smiling at her. The next moment he flung his arms up into the air, in utter enjoyment of the moment, as if celebrating life. She was still waving at him when the fender of an enormous truck filled the background. It closed in fast, crushing him between itself and the Kombi.'

Anthon took a deep breath, his eyes giving away he was living the moment as if he'd experienced it himself.

'The driver of the truck had fallen asleep behind the steering wheel. Ben died instantly.' His voice tightened with sorrow.

'Lisa was six months pregnant with their first child.'

The half-moon rose behind the distant mountains, its cold metallic sheen creating mysterious shapes, groping at the shadows brought to life by the flickering flames of our fire.

'Lisa brought Ben's ashes back to Namibia. I arranged everything, as I had promised him that evening, here in this same desert. We were a convoy of vehicles. He had many friends. It took quite a bit of logistical planning to get them all here, to feed them, to figure out where to camp, so I asked one of the local tour guides to organise the trip for me.'

A gush of cold air wafted in from the coast. Anthon wrapped his arm around my shoulders, drawing me closer to his warmth.

'We scattered his ashes on that same small mountain top, not far from here. When we left, the strangest thing happened. The tour guide, another close friend and I were the last to leave. As we drove off, the tour guide glanced back. "Did we leave anyone behind?" he asked, perplexed. "No," I answered. "Why?"'

'"I can swear there's someone still standing on the *koppie*," he replied, shaking his head. I looked in my rear-view mirror and saw the silhouette of a tall man standing on the rocks, dark against the blue of the sky, waving. I knew it was Ben. To my astonishment, my friend replied, "Don't worry, it's only Ben. He won't be coming back with us."

'The tour guide looked back again, dumbfounded, but the figure was gone.'

'When did Ben die?' My logical mind wanted to create a timeline, to bring back structure to the story, to chase away the shadows on the edge of my field of vision.

'More than twelve years ago,' he replied, his voice pensive.

'Did you ever come back here?'

'No. Nobody wanted to venture so far from civilisation with me.'

I slept fitfully that night. I expected this northern part of the Namib to be full of soothing night sounds, jackal calls, the screech of cicadas, like in the Southern Namib. Here, on the edge of the Skeleton Coast, the stillness was absolute, even oppressive. It invaded my dreams. I spent the night struggling with my own demons, tormenting me in ways which seemed indescribable and ridiculous by daylight.

The next morning we rose before the sun, packed up our camp and removed all traces of the fire and our presence. The desert is unforgiving and carries its scars for decades, sometimes centuries. We like to leave it as we found it, to tread as lightly on this eternity as we possibly can.

Barely one kilometre from where we camped, we came upon a fountain. The Ougams Fountain, as Anthon explained. Animal tracks patterned the mud surrounding the pool of water, yet I couldn't remember seeing or hearing another living thing since our arrival the previous evening. The sun was still below the horizon. Ribbons of cloud streaked the sky, its violet hue reflecting in the quiet pond. On closer inspection the glassy surface teemed with tiny insect larvae, their flying counterparts hovering slightly above. Delicate concentric circles betrayed where water trickled into the pond. We followed the rivulet to its source, hidden amongst a few rocks. It appeared modest, even insignificant.

'Impressive!' I said. 'To think this humble gurgle is the only constant fountain for many, many miles.'

'One must be careful never to camp too close to a water hole, especially in an area as dry as this,' Anthon said.

'Because of snakes, I suppose?' I asked.

'Perhaps that could be an added motivation,' he laughed. 'A human presence in the vicinity of a water source will discourage animals from approaching. These creatures walk for days to satisfy their thirst. They could die if they're not able to drink.'

'Makes sense to me.' I agreed.

We continued south, diligently following the two-track path. It led us into a valley protected by rocky outcrops on both sides. Leaving the spoor made by the vehicles which preceded you is regarded as sacrilege, as disrespect for this pristine piece of wilderness. From the lightness of the two tracks rolling out in front of us, it was clear that few vehicles ventured this way.

To my eye, most of the *koppies* on either side of us looked alike.

'How on earth are you going to find the exact place where you scattered Ben's ashes?' I didn't believe for a moment he'd find it again, after such a long time.

'I'll find it.' His self-assurance was unwavering.

'How would you know it's the place anyway?' I asked. 'Did you leave a memorial plaque or some other marker?'

'No, we didn't put up anything,' he answered, 'but I'll know.'

'Ja, ja,' I said to myself. Did it matter anyway? The spectacular surroundings were reason enough to be there.

Without warning he brought Henry to a halt.

'This is it,' triumph written all over his face.

We left Henry on the track, so as not to make any new markings on the valley floor. The chances of anybody else using this path within the next few days were slim. With apprehension, I followed Anthon to the foot of a ridge, some distance from the Land Rover, towards the west. The valley was still in shadow, the sky illuminated by the amber and rose preceding sunrise. As we started to climb higher, the sun emerged behind the inland *koppies* to the east, banishing all gloom. The uppermost granite boulders glowed liquid copper. Halfway up the hill, I passed a desert shrub which could've been straight from a science fiction movie. Its swollen, gnarled and pitted grey trunk was topped with fleshy fingerlike leaves on short fat branches. If eyes and a mouth appeared on closer inspection, I wouldn't have blinked an eye.

'An Elephant's Foot,' Anthon informed me. Of course! A more apt name couldn't have been given to this particular plant in this magical environment.

Reaching the top, I was stunned by the beauty of this fragile land. Looking back into the valley, Henry had turned into a speck in the bottom of what now resembled a wide riverbed. Far grander mountains and plains extended in all directions away from us. To the west, a distant bank of blue-grey fog betrayed the position of the far-off coastline. Walking along the ridge, I suspected that Anthon wasn't as sure about this being the place as he appeared to be down in the valley. Spellbound by the vistas, I'd no idea what to look for, if anything. Yet, on reaching the far end of the ridge, I was the one to stumble upon something.

'Did somebody leave a marker here?' I called to Anthon.

'Not that I know of,' he replied, 'but I'll come and have a look anyway.'

There was no doubt about it. This was the place. A flimsy wooden cross, barely thirty centimetres high, wedged between two rocks. Ben's name and the dates of his birth and death were scribbled on it with a ballpoint pen. We would find out much later that his sister put it up, but at least we were sure it was the right location.

As we sat down on the rock next to the tiny memorial, we made the most wondrous discovery. Directly below the cross, a tiny heap of minuscule bone particles lay in a hollow in the rock. Without question the heavier remains of Ben's ashes, which couldn't be blown away by the wind. Untouched for twelve years.

'The eternal desert,' I thought, 'how appropriate.'

By now the sun was up. The granite rocks sighed and crackled as the first heat of the day expanded their surfaces.

'Don't you think this is a splendid venue for a breakfast?' Anthon suggested.

I needed no persuasion. He fetched our small gas stove, our two-cup percolator, a bottle of water and two mugs, while I carried the condensed milk, the ground coffee and the rusks. We clambered back onto the *koppie.* He lit the flame behind a rock and set up the percolator. Soon we were dunking rusks into mugs of steaming coffee, the endlessness of creation stretched out below us.

'Ben would've approved,' Anthon remarked with satisfaction.

As if from nowhere, a single yellow butterfly appeared and perched itself upon the nearby Elephant's Foot.

Chapter 13

A PETRIFIED POLAR BEAR ON THE EDGE OF THE SKELETON COAST

From here the track wound lightly over a sandy valley guarded on both sides by rock formations, sculpted through millennia by wind, sun and occasionally, rain. A lone oryx pair regarded us with astonishment. I, in turn, wondered what they grazed upon in this barren valley with no visible sustenance or water.

'Oryx are amazing creatures, perfectly adapted to the arid parts of Namibia,' Anthon answered my thought. 'They can endure extreme temperatures. They even developed their own air con system.'

'How?' I asked.

'In much the same way a modern water cooler lowers the air temperature in a room,' he chuckled. I pinched my mouth, wondering whether he got me yet again.

'It's quite simple,' he sounded earnest enough. 'The animal has a biological cooler system in its nose. While breathing fast, blood is pumped through its snout, which lowers its blood temperature and prevents it from losing moisture when it breathes.'

Anthon started searching for something between his seat and the centre glove compartment. He found a book, which he handed to me.

'See what they say in this guide about oryx,' he instructed.

I leafed through the pages, which contained fascinating facts about the Namibian desert and its creatures.

'Wow!', I exclaimed, 'an oryx can breathe as fast as 210 times a minute. According to this book, its body temperature can reach more than 40 degrees Celsius while its brain stays much cooler.' I closed the book, keeping my finger between the pages as a place marker.

'Surely they still need water?' I visualised the oryx we'd encountered in the Southern Namib, at Sossusvlei, where it seldom rained.

'It's precisely because of its high body temperature that it conserves moisture. It can survive for long periods without drinking any water at all,' he explained.

'I don't understand.' I felt a bit dumb. I never had much

interest in physiology. 'What's its high body temperature got to do with water conservation?'

'We sweat to cool down our bodies. Talk your own language and think air conditioner, *Mein Schatz,*' he laughed. 'If it doesn't sweat, because its body regards this higher body temperature as normal, it doesn't lose precious moisture. It can survive on the liquid obtained from a few wild melons or other tubers. But they go even further. To conserve more liquid, they can concentrate their urine and excrete the uric acid as crystals.'

'Are you trying to tell me they pee solids?' I asked, opening the book to check whether he was mocking me.

'Unbelievable!' I confirmed, 'and furthermore, their bellies are white to reflect the heat rising from the desert.'

'I grew up in the Kalahari, *Mein Schatz,* like these animals, I also had to develop survival skills,' he chuckled.

'I'm starting to feel guilty about that oryx fillet we had last night,' I replied, a bit mortified. 'They're perfectly adapted to survive in the desert, but are helpless against humans with hunting rifles.'

'Don't feel too bad. Albie showed me what happens when there are more oryx on his farm than the vegetation can handle. Now and again, when a few have to be culled, we're lucky enough to get oryx fillet for dinner.'

We'd been crawling uphill, as the valley floor rose away from the Ougams fountain and the riverbed where we'd spent the night. Now we were approaching the watershed.

'Let's see what the view over the valley looks like from those boulders. There's something I want to show you,' Anthon suggested, slowing Henry to a standstill.

We walked the fifty meters to the pile of rounded boulders, the remains of an ancient granite massif. Cracked, stacked and polished as if by a giant. The early morning sun was already stinging the bare patch at the back of my neck. As our vantage point rose, we could see over the watershed and into the valley beyond. The two light tracks we'd been following since yesterday, faded into a thick eiderdown of fog hovering above the valley floor, obscuring any view of what lay further ahead.

Anthon peered into the distance. 'You probably won't believe me, but I thought we might be able to get a glimpse of the polar bear.'

'The what?' I assumed I must've heard him incorrectly.

'Never mind. Let's see what pops out of the mist down below. We'll now be gradually descending towards the Khumib Valley,' he changed the subject. 'Hold thumbs the river hadn't come down during the heavy inland rains of the last few days.'

'Is the Khumib as large as the Hoarusib?' I asked.

'It doesn't really depend on the size of the river. When it floods, humans and their vehicles wait.'

Back in Henry, I opened the map we permanently keep between the seats.

'Interesting,' I said. 'I hadn't realised that the Hoarusib, which we already crossed at Otjiu, only reaches the Atlantic Ocean thirty or so kilometres south of the Khumib.'

'There's a mountain range in between, running roughly parallel to the coast,' Anthon explained what I saw on the map.

'The Hoarusib has its source much further to the north-west, but the mountain blocks its direct passage to the sea, so it first flows south until it reaches an opening to the coast. The Khumib originates on the western side of this mountain range and flows more directly to the ocean.'

By now we were entering the fog, not half as dense as it appeared from a distance. A flaxen radiance lit the sculpted valley as the swirling and rising vapour absorbed the sunlight. Hazy outlines of granite boulders brooded in the mist.

All of a sudden a massive figure appeared ahead of us. Anthon slowed Henry down to a crawl.

'The Polar Bear!' He looked at me with a smug grin, as Henry jolted to a halt.

My heart did a tumble as my brain tried to make sense of the image appearing out of the fog. For a moment I was convinced it was a real polar bear. The colossal body, head slightly lowered, was a perfect granite replica of the animal. Coming across this vision, in this primordial landscape, not having seen another human being for at least 24 hours, was surreal. This time I didn't reach for my camera. Some souvenirs can only be carried deep inside. Or chiselled with words, many years later.

'Now you know why we refer to this track as the Bear Road. You're lucky, *Mein Schatz*, few people have the privilege of ever coming this way.'

As we drove past the Polar Bear rock formation, I looked back. From this angle, the resemblance was even more uncanny.

'A petrified polar bear on the edge of the Skeleton Coast. Who'd believe me?' I said.

Anthon laughed.

'It reminds me of the stories I used to tell the girls to keep them occupied during long journeys, when they were still small,' I added.

'You're a storyteller as well as an architect?'

'I love making up stories,' I replied, unperturbed. 'One of

their favourites was about the dinosaur turned into stone by a mean magician, a tale I wove around the rocky outcrops one finds in the Southern Namib. Don't you agree they often resemble the finny backs of ancient creatures, lurking half under the sand, waiting to shake off their enchantment and transform back to life?'

'Now that you paint it so vividly, I must admit I can also picture it,' he conceded.

'Of course, most of the stories included a liberal sprinkle of wizards, witches and magic,' I continued. 'Sometimes the dinosaur was a dragon, which terrorised the countryside and therefore deserved its fate as a heap of boulders. Mostly the spells were reversible. The innocent mountain range or rocky ridge might wake up at any time, shake the sand off its back and revert to its ancient reptilian shape.'

'So that's why you enjoy reading stories to me when we drive to Cape Town?' Anthon joked.

'I'm still going to write one as well,' I returned the joke.

From here the *spoor* meandered over expanses of gritty orange sand, forming miniature plains flanked by granite ridges. The sun, now fully visible, had chased all the mist back to its source at the coast, where the cold Benguela current created an icy breeze as it clashed with the hot, thirsty air rising from the desert. We stopped to admire a spiny Candelabra Euphorbia, which is toxic to most animals, yet rhinos can graze on it to their hearts' delight. Their mouths must be as hard as the soles of our shoes not to be cut by the vicious spines of the succulent. I wished I had my macro lens with me. I would've loved taking close-ups of the barbs.

Rounding yet another granite boulder, we abruptly

reached what appeared to be a T-junction and the end of our track. The Khumib River Valley lay before us.

Before descending into the riverbed we stopped to scan the surroundings. Although no running water or puddles were visible, the river clearly must have come down recently. In places, the sand still appeared damp and a bit of flood debris was strewn about. Recent tyre tracks indicated a vehicle had passed this way after the flood.

'Fortunately the road seems passable,' Anthon concluded. 'It usually runs in the riverbed, where it's sandy, but generally there's a secondary track on higher ground as well. This is the road to the Skeleton Coast tourist concessions, but without a permit we may not travel much further towards the west. The park isn't fenced, but the boundary is close by. If one of the rangers finds you inside the park without a permit, you can get a hefty fine.'

We proceeded into the riverbed until we reached the sandy track, still damp, but solid under Henry's wheels. From here we turned inland. Tracking the path of the watercourse, we wound our way around rocks and the occasional tree stump dumped by previous floods.

'Giraffes!' I spotted two comical, fluffy-horned heads on long necks peering inquisitively at us over the vegetation lining the riverbed. 'May we stop and look at them?'

'As good a spot as any to have a cup of coffee,' Anthon agreed. 'They seem to find us just as interesting.'

Ten minutes later we were sitting on meandering ripples of river sand, a cup of coffee in one hand and a rusk in the other. A herd of giraffes grazed lazily, not twenty meters away. The rustle of branches was audible as they tore leaves off the Acacia trees with their leathery lips. One could even hear the scrunching of teeth as they munched away, all the while keeping their huge, long-lashed eyes on us. Their other movements were soundless. It was only when a few youngsters started a chasing game that a soft clattering of hooves became audible.

'Part of the magic of travelling this far from civilisation,' Anthon observed. 'The animals are completely unperturbed by our presence.'

We reluctantly left them behind to continue our journey.

By the time we reached the much more frequented D3707, which we'd left so abruptly the day before, the sun was close to its zenith.

'Back in civilisation,' Anthon joked. 'Are you ready for a possible encounter with something of the vehicular kind?'

'What a shock to the system!' I exclaimed. A convoy of three off-road vehicles hurried by in a cloud of dust, as if summoned by his words. 'We seem to have hit rush hour traffic.'

'I must tell you this story.' Anthon shifted his weight in his seat, collecting a yarn from his memory bank. I decided to make myself comfortable as well. It had been some time since we'd had one of his anecdotes.

'A couple of years ago, before cell phones became mandatory accessories, I arrived at a lodge near Sesriem to do their annual medicals. The manager, Chris, was a good friend of mine. He joined me for a beer. I could see he was stressed out.'

'"Doc," he said to me, "I think I've now seen everything."'

'"What do you mean, everything?" I asked as I opened my bottle of ice cold Erdinger. "Tourists, my dear doctor, overseas tourists," Chris lamented, woefully shaking his head. "Five days ago, these French tourists arrived at the lodge." He took a long sip from his beer bottle. "Husband and wife. Probably mid-sixties." He took another sip. I knew it was going to be a long story. But I had time,' Anthon chuckled.

'"Having hired a vehicle at the airport, they drove south to Aus, where they spent the night," Chris continued his saga. "The next day they drove from Aus on the gravel road towards Helmeringhauzen, then turned west onto the D707 to Sesriem. But all this I only found out later."'

'The scenic road on the edge of the red dunes?' I interrupted Anthon's story.

'Yes,' he confirmed. 'Panoramic, but not in the best condition and badly signposted. Not the preferred route for anyone in a hurry.' He lit a cigarette, hanging his hand out of the window to prevent the smoke from entering the car.

'Anyway,' he continued, 'after having heard what road they took, I assumed they must've had a couple of punctures, didn't know how to fix them or didn't carry any water.' He shrugged his shoulders as he looked at me. 'You know, the normal problems encountered by foreign tourists driving in the remoter parts of Namibia for the first time. They look at a map, see a line denoting a road, a dot with a name next to it, and assume the road will lead to a town where one can fill your tank or maybe get a cup of coffee. When I said as much to Chris, his face fell even further.'

'"No, Doc, believe me, they didn't have a single mishap," he answered. "They drove slowly, which spared them any punctures. They had food. They had water. They hired a decent off-road vehicle, but when they arrived here at our lodge in the evening they were completely traumatised."'

'Then he said nothing. He just sat there, downing his beer, looking equally traumatised himself. I had to prod him to tell me what had happened. "Doc, give me time, it's a long story. I'm getting there." He called the barman and ordered a second beer before he continued. "Front office called me, as they couldn't understand a word the tourists were saying. Them being French, their English erratic, to say the least, and their German non-existent, we communicated with hands, arms, legs, whatever. I was so agitated I even chucked in some Damara by accident. I gathered they wanted to go back to Windhoek immediately. In the meantime I asked my maintenance manager to have a look at the car, to see whether they may have had an accident, perhaps rolled the car or something, but he came back shaking his head. The car was in perfect condition." By this time I decided not to rush him. I also ordered a second beer, prepared to wait for the punchline. Another half-a-beer later, Chris proceeded with his tale: "I finally persuaded the tourists to allow reception to book them in and take their luggage to their room. While the porter fetched their bags, I took them to the bar and poured them both a triple brandy and coke." Here I started to worry that Chris would also order one, but by now he was on a roll. "I then had a brain wave," Chris continued, "I called Jacques, my French neighbour, to come and help. By the time he arrived, they were getting a bit tipsy, because I'd poured them a second brandy and coke, only realising afterwards they might not have eaten much during the day. I wish you could've seen their faces when Jacques greeted them in French. I expected them to jump up and down and wag their tails like puppies whose people had just arrived home from work." Of course, I couldn't let that opportunity pass and asked Chris whether they rolled over and peed on the carpet as well, but ol' Chris was so engrossed in his recollection he didn't catch my attempt at a joke and just pushed on with his story.'

'"My guests started talking rapidly. All in French, of course," Chris continued. "They were agitated and waved their hands and arms about. Jacques' eyes grew wider and wider and his face got this funny expression. Knowing my friend well, I realised the bugger was going to burst out laughing. I had to make a plan; create a diversion. I knocked over my own glass of beer and sent Jacques to the bar to get a cloth from the waiter. I could see the *Arschloch* folding double with laughter from where I was sitting, but fortunately the Frenchies had their backs to him. At least he had himself under control when he came back. Doc, I'm telling you, you've never heard anything like this. I called a porter to accompany them to their room to freshen up before dinner. Just to get them out of the way. When they were gone I asked Jacques to tell me what the fuck was going on. He told me they…" — and then Chris gave a snort — "… they drove from Aus…" — here he started laughing so much he could hardly talk —, "…onto the C14…" — by now his tears were running — "…then onto the D707. And by that time they hadn't seen a single vehicle." — Here Chris lost it completely. I thought he was hysterical —. "They started panicking, convinced they were lost. And on the D707 there's nothing. No buildings, people, vehicles, towns or signposts. They paid a fortune to be flown out of here the next day, Doc. I had to get the car rental company to come and collect their car. They believe they were at death's door."'

'"Doc," he said as he wiped the tears from his eyes, "I'm telling you, I've now seen everything." Anthon paused; by now Chris's story had him out of breath.

I was too flabbergasted to laugh. 'They were traumatised because they didn't see any sign of people, any human imprint, except for the road, for the entire day?' I asked in total disbelief.

'Exactly,' Anthon confirmed, also laughing by now. 'They apparently started telling each other how they were lost on a deserted road, how they probably took the wrong turn off, how there could be dangerous wild animals, how they'd die of exposure should anything happen to the car, how other vehicles probably only pass that way once a month. By late afternoon they'd worked each other into a frenzy.'

'The car had no GPS?' I asked, but already knew the answer.

'No, that was before a GPS was an affordable accessory,' Anthon answered. 'They were completely stressed out by demons entirely of their own creation. Something humans are extremely good at doing. Come to think of it, humans are probably the only species capable of making their own lives a misery simply by using their imaginations.'

I also started laughing. 'I can write a book about imagined fears, which never came to pass. Most of them from personal experience.'

After having driven along the Bear Road, the plain we drove through now was magnificent in its utter desolation. An ochre rock-strewn infinity quivered against the distant mountains.

'Can we please stop?' I asked.

As always, he obliged. Grabbing my camera, I clambered out of Henry and walked away from the road, giving the dust time to blow away. I kneeled on the gravel. Still not low enough, I lay down flat on my belly, aiming my camera from the lowest level and widest angle I could muster. How does one capture eternity on film? Rocks were strewn at random. Some were blurred by their closeness to my lens. Others marched silently into the distance with a grotesquely distorted perspective, dwarfing the faraway purple mountains which trembled with the heat rising from the fiery earth.

'I swear I can feel the heartbeat of the planet thumping through my body,' I declared dramatically when Anthon joined me, my hat in his hand.

'More likely you're experiencing the first throbbing of heatstroke, *Mein Schatz.* You once again left your hat in the car,' he scolded. I allowed him to put it on my head, not looking forward to another unbearable migraine due to too much sun and no head covering. Not to mention the painful after-effects of sunburn.

On my way back to Henry, I couldn't resist picking up a few scorched and wind scoured pebbles, some so hot they burned my hands. These would form part of our memory bank. We're hoarders. No amount of therapy can rehabilitate us. We love to haul bits and pieces back to our lair, our *stoep* in Windhoek. Our justification? It was beautiful. Or strange. Or sculptural. Even its texture could be the pretext. It gives us a further reason to buy handmade crafts from the local inhabitants in the exotic places we pass through: Finely patterned straw baskets found in Kavango, hand-carved wooden bowls collected in the Caprivi, earthy wood-fired clay vessels from Rundu, huge mahango storage baskets spotted next to the road in Ovamboland; all to serve as containers for our hoarded treasures. These, in turn, trigger memories, recall places and help us to relive our journeys.

Chapter 14

INVISIBLE AND IMAGINARY DESERT ELEPHANTS

The next dot on the map was named Puros.

'How far to Puros?' I asked. 'And how big is the town?'

'If you expect a town, you're in for a disappointment. It's only slightly larger than Orupembe,' Anthon laughed. 'But we're about fifteen kilometres away from it.'

'So again only a small shop?' I wondered.

'A little more. There's a Himba settlement as well. And a community campsite. Doing Kaokoland is popular with Namibian and South African off-road enthusiasts. You need a sturdy, reliable four-wheel drive vehicle and good equipment to travel to these parts. The tourism industry helped the locals to establish a number of community campsites, especially in Damaraland and Kaokoland. They offer basic facilities, such as water, long drop toilets and a flat area to camp and light a fire. The campsite at Puros is a popular stopover amongst self-drive tourists.'

The topography now contrasted wildly with the red plains we passed through barely fifteen minutes ago. We'd started the descent into the massive Hoarusib Valley. The escarpment dropped away in front of us; scrunched up and folded like an ochre leather shammy left in the sun to dry.

It was the hour after midday, the heat unbearable. Henry didn't boast modern accessories, such as temperature gauges, but it could've easily been in the mid to high forties. Driving with the windows open allowed a measure of airflow over our perspiring bodies, although it felt more like a blast from a furnace than a cooling breeze.

I noticed Anthon was constantly glancing into his rear-view mirror.

'Anything the matter?' I asked.

'There's a vehicle behind us, flashing his lights at me. It doesn't feel as though I've got a flat tyre. I suppose I'll have to pull over and hear what the problem is.'

A Toyota, a macho, wide rimmed machine with chromium plated bull bars, a snorkel, two extra tyres and loads of shiny trim, slid to a halt in a cloud of dust next to us. The driver opened his electric passenger window and glared at us through wraparound reflective sunglasses, aggressively waving a packet of potato chips at us.

'We don't need your type here in the Kaokoland!' he shouted, without greeting. 'You're the tourist-scum who messes up our environment with your rubbish.' With that he chucked the packet into our vehicle, rolled up his window and roared off, leaving us spluttering in another smother of fine red dust particles.

Turning around in my seat, I saw that our snack bag on the back seat had blown open. Unbeknown to us, the turbulence caused inside the car by the open windows must've whirled it out of the back window.

'Why on earth would anyone purposefully throw a perfectly good, sealed packet of chips out of their car, miles from civilisation, with no hope of replacing it for a couple of days?' I spluttered, when I finally managed to gulp a clean breath of air again. 'Yes, it's ours, but we had no idea we lost it.' I was furious.

'Don't ask. His wife probably left him for a guy with a Land Rover.' Anthon boomed with laughter. He always saw the lighter side.

'What a righteous, miserable man!' I couldn't help adding.

'I've been called that once. And to my face,' Anthon chuckled.

'Really? By whom?' I asked. His tactics worked again. My anger dissipated at once, eager to hear another story.

'She was a diminutive old lady; must've been around 81 years old. Let's call her Mrs G. She was Very English. Still spoke the Queen's language the proper way, you know.' He affected the British pronunciation made famous by James Bond, illustrating his exceptional knack for accents.

'I was working as a medical officer at the Spinal Cord Unit of a well known Cape Town hospital, now unfortunately no longer in existence. Mrs G had severe osteoarthritis in her spine and all her joints, caused by an old whiplash injury she sustained when someone drove into the back of her car many years before. I had to treat her for Central Cord Syndrome.'

'Explain?' I requested. Studying illnesses on the internet isn't one of my hobbies, so my medical knowledge is patchy, to say the least.

'It's a strange condition,' he explained, 'which leaves the sufferer's legs with movement, but no sensation and conversely leaves their hands with sensation, but no movement. It's a bizarre illness. It gives and takes. We always say it gives where you don't want it and takes where you do want it: movement without feeling, and feeling without movement.'

'Anyway, as a result of her disease, the poor old girl suffered from chronic pain and was on a myriad of NSAID's.'

'There you go again. What are NS-what-evers?' I had to laugh at my own ignorance regarding matters medical.

'Non-steroidal anti-inflammatory medications.' His patience was unlimited; up to a certain point, anyway. 'We call them NSAID's, for short. Now, you must understand, these medications can cause gastric bleeds in healthy patients; in those already suffering from spinal cord injuries they're dangerous.'

'Every morning as I did my ward rounds, I'd ask Mrs G how she was and every morning she'd complain bitterly of the terrible pain in her limbs and body. Due to her condition I never even considered giving her NSAID's. I also couldn't give her opioids, as other than causing severe constipation, it causes dependency. Not that she wasn't dependent on her NSAID's, but that was more of a psychological attachment; opioids would cause a physical addiction. So my only option was to give her paracetamol.'

'Of course, she wasn't impressed. I explained the possible side effects and complications of the alternative pain medications to her *ad nauseam,* but she refused to budge. I could sense her growing resentment towards me. One morning, as I arrived next to her bed, she was ready, waiting for me. Sitting upright, she couldn't contain her irritation any longer.'

'"Dr Schröder,"' she said, looking straight in front of her. Tight-lipped; refusing to make eye contact. "You're a miserable man." Her entire manner shouted: "I've finally said what I wanted to say. Now go away! Leave me in peace to suffer by myself."'

'"Mrs G," I answered, "do you think I'm not acutely aware of just how miserable I am? I've got to live with myself 24 hours a day, seven days a week. Do you know what that feels like? Don't you feel sorry for me?" I took her hand and pressed it. Still staring in front of her, I could see her shoulders softening and a twinkle appearing in her blue eyes. The next morning, when I asked her how her pain was, she turned towards me and looked straight at me. Then, with a slight flutter of her lashes, she said to me: "you're the expert, the doctor. You know all about my pain. I shouldn't have to tell you." From then on we were friends.

'What happened to her?' I wanted to know. 'Can such a condition be treated?'

'That spinal unit was primarily a rehabilitation facility. We taught patients how to live with their conditions. After the initial treatment, the patients started a program where they received intensive therapy from physio- and occupational therapists,' Anthon answered.

He spoke from experience. He chose to work in this particular spinal hospital after his own encounter with paralysis. During his housemanship year in Windhoek, they had to perform an emergency Caesarean on a 130kg lady. It was late at night and the porter, who had to help to move the patient from the trolley onto the operating table, was nowhere to be found. As the mother and the unborn baby were in severe danger, Anthon moved the patient himself. In the process, he twisted his back. The next morning he woke with severe back pain. When you're a houseman, if you can still stand upright, you go to work. He went to a colleague in the orthopaedic department and told him what had happened. His friend examined him and put him on the next flight to Cape Town, to see a neurosurgeon. By then he had a 'drop foot', the first phase of paralysis in his leg. After a back operation and three months of rehabilitation, he could return to work. This episode left such an impression on him he decided to spend time working in the spinal hospital. He retained a life long interest in treating and rehabilitating spinal cord injuries.

'Mrs G's story had a lovely ending, though,' Anthon said, a wicked grin on his face.

'There was an old gentleman who came to see her regularly while she was in the hospital. He used to be a physiotherapist. He was concerned about her rehabilitation program and told her he wanted to make sure the young physio's treated her correctly. One day, she called me aside.'

'"Dr Schröder," she murmured, while glancing around the room to make sure nobody was eavesdropping on us, "I thought Mr H just came to see me to check on my progress, but now I suspect he might have… — she cupped her hand next to her mouth and started to whisper —, …you know, ulterior motives." She turned towards me with her large blue eyes, to stress the gravity of this possibility.'

'"And why would you think that, Mrs G?" I asked her, my eyes equally large and innocent.'

'"He comes all the way from Silvermine to this hospital, Doctor, and that's more than one and a half hour's drive. Once a week!" She looked vindicated. She'd caught him out.'

'"Mrs G," I said, "How wonderful that you can still summon men to your bed at the age of 81."'

'"Don't be silly, Doctor," she said, blushing like a teenager. "Seriously now, what must I do about it? Must I tell him to go away?"'

'Over the next few weeks I could see a change in her, until one morning she patted the bed next to her, inviting me to sit down. "This is now getting serious, Doctor," she informed me with wide eyes. I took her hand. "Talk to me," I said. She looked like a young girl, in love for the first time and too scared to tell her parents about it.'

'"He wants us to get engaged, Doctor," she confided, "but I can't possibly marry him. He's only 75!"'

'And? Was there a happy ending?' I laughed.

'Of course!' Anthon replied. 'Three months later they were married. When I saw her again she said to me, contentedly, "Doctor, I'm the envy of all my friends, as well as of all those women I don't like.' She winked at me.

As Mrs G's story unfolded, we'd been descending into the Hoarusib River Valley. The reddish-brown gravel abruptly stopped at the bottom of the valley, where a band of mottled green traced the line of the watercourse. On the other side, a straw coloured landscape rose into another barren massif, now hazed by the dusty distance. It was well past midday. The heat baked into the earth, then rose in tremors and shudders, drawing in cold air from the faraway

Atlantic. Regrettably, by the time it reached Puros, this west wind had whipped up the desert heat and sand, offering no reprieve. It merely pulled a film of grey over the landscape. In the distance, a few mud coloured structures grew from the soil.

'Puros,' Anthon confirmed. 'But, if you don't mind, I'd prefer to push on. I'd like us to camp at Palmwag tonight, and that's still at least two hours from here.'

The heat pounded me with a sledgehammer. I could feel the perspiration running down my back. I had no desire to explore Puros. On reaching the riverbed, the road disappeared. We halted, leaving the engine to idle.

Anthon peered over the expanse of sand, broken by islands where flood debris decorated rocks and vegetation with twigs and silt.

'It did come down recently but has dried up again. Let's look for the best place to cross.'

We drove a short way along the river's edge. In places the sand was covered by a thin layer of silt, dried and cracked into a carpet of potato chips. We spotted the spoor of previous vehicles.

'Might as well take this one,' he decided. 'Now hold on tight. The sand is quite soft and we might hit thick patches. Once I'm in, there's no stopping until we're through. Okay?'

Henry is the most marvellous vehicle on rugged terrain, but he's heavy. Anthon readily concedes a Defender isn't the best choice when it comes to driving on sand.

'So no stopping for photographs?' I was a bit disappointed. I was looking forward to a wide shot from the middle of the river.

'No stopping. Full stop,' was his firm answer.

He put Henry into first gear, made sure he was in

donkey — the local lingo for low range —, then eased the vehicle over the incline and onto the sand. The first channel was easy, but as we swerved around a huge Ana tree, we found ourselves in the middle of a patch of silt flakes. Dust whirled all around us. I struggled to wind up my window. We reached the other river bank coughing and sneezing.

'This crossing can be a nightmare in the dry season,' Anthon explained, once back on the road. 'When the silt dries, it forms a fine powder, which collects into dust bowls. Sometimes they're massive. I've seen a vehicle disappear up to its chassis into one of those in the Khowareb Schlucht.'

On the other side of the river, the road was light coloured and sandy, in stark contrast to the reddish brown surface we'd driven on earlier. The landscape was also less barren, sprinkled with straw coloured grass and shrubs. Scattered trees fought the elements for their existence, their weathered branches clawing against the azure sky.

Anthon slowed the vehicle down. 'Look there! On the right-hand side of the road. Can you see it?'

'Are those elephant footprints?' I asked. A single file of tracks as large as dinner plates marked the fine dust on the edge of the road.

'There's your answer,' Anthon pointed to a hill of fresh dung. 'You might be lucky, *Mein Schatz,* and see your first desert elephant.'

I sat up straight and scoured the landscape. I relived my first childhood trip to the Kruger National Park.

Faraway a thin line of Acacias marked another water run-off, discharging into the river behind us.

Every distant bush or rock was ready to sprout a trunk and a pair of tusks.

A couple of springbok stared at me. 'What's your problem?' they seemed to ask.

Kilometres passed. My impatience grew with every fresh sign next to the road.

Nothing.

'Surely an elephant is too large to vanish in such a sparse environment?' I asked.

'I must admit, I don't see any either,' Anthon agreed, 'but here is yet another sign.'

He pointed to a green Acacia branch, torn off a nearby tree and discarded in the middle of the road. Again we strained our eyes, constantly searching the veldt as we drove, but all we saw were more tracks, heaps of fresh dung, leaves, twigs. Like that kid in Kruger, so many years ago, my interest waned.

'Remember last year's trip, when we decided to camp in the Ugab?' I reminisced instead.

'When you were so afraid an elephant might carry you off during the night?' Anthon's devils danced again.

I smiled at the recollection. I had to do a site visit for yet another government feasibility, this time located in an inaccessible part of Damaraland.

'You're a master at fabricating excuses to turn work into a camping trip, aren't you?' I returned the jibe.

'You yourself admitted you don't fancy driving off-road. If I recall correctly the road to that site was horrendous. It would've been irresponsible of me to allow you to go on your own,' he defended himself. 'And,' he paused to emphasise the death blow, 'you refuse to drive Henry.'

I rubbed his knee. 'And I always appreciate your concern and love your company. Especially if we can squeeze a camping trip into the bargain. Come to think of it, I love you, full stop!' And so I won again.

'I was prevented from collecting one of my own rooftop tents from the Previous Dispensation. So we bought that new dome tent,' Anthon remembered. 'Why did everything happen in such a rush again? Why did I ask Titus to get our camping gear ready instead of doing it myself, as I normally do?'

'It was all due to that late appointment by the Ministry of Works,' I answered. 'As usual, they waited until the fiscal year was just about over. When they realised some of the feasibilities budgeted for that financial year were still outstanding, Officialdom dumped the problem onto a couple of consultants. I needed the work, so I said, 'Yes Sir, Thank You Sir' and obliged. You were fully booked for the two days before we left. I had to collect all the site information, attend the briefing and buy our provisions.'

'You're right. And we still lived in separate houses at the time.'

'You asked Titus to pack all the camping stuff in Henry so we could leave before dawn the next day. We only had the food to pack when you picked me up from my place,' I refreshed his memory.

We left at first light and drove directly to the site, only stopping along the way for a quick bite to eat. Arriving around lunchtime, I managed to complete my investigation within two hours.

Late afternoon, we descended with the sun into the Ugab Valley. The community campsites are scattered under giant Ana trees on the bank of the dry riverbed. It was deserted. We parked Henry under a tree and Anthon went in search of whoever was in charge. While he was gone, I opened

Henry's tap and splashed my face and arms with water. The heat in the valley was suffocating, in spite of the sun already being nearly gone. He returned with the caretaker, a corpulent *meme* in a richly patterned Herero dress.

After the customary greeting, she explained to us we could pitch our tent wherever we wanted to. She didn't expect any other campers that evening. Then she pointed in the direction of a reed shelter some distance from where we parked Henry.

'The *abrution brock*,' she clarified.

'But *preese*, Tate, watch out for the *erephants*!' she added.

'When last did the elephants come through the camp?' I asked, somewhat concerned.

'Eeeeh, not today, *meme*, but perhaps the day before that.'

She walked towards the riverbed, waving her arm to describe a wide curve, 'but they *rike* to walk here at night,' she answered.

I looked around furtively, just to make sure one wasn't sneaking up on us.

'Have you got any *olanges*?' she asked.

'No *meme*,' Anthon smiled at my incomprehension, 'we didn't bring any oranges or other fruit. We know the elephants will dig into our stuff for those.' She nodded, pleased.

'And be *carefur* of the bees as well,' she added as she left, looking towards Henry's back door.

'The bees?' I asked Anthon.

'Wow, look at the activity around Henry's tap!' I noticed the hum for the first time. The wet soil underneath the tap was vibrating with black and yellow life.

'They should start disappearing after sunset,' he replied, unconcerned. He filled a plate with water and put it a couple of meters away from the vehicle. 'This might tempt them away from us. They're thirsty. The veldt is bone dry.' The first rains of the season hadn't yet fallen here.

'And the elephants?' I asked. I've got a lot of respect for wild animals. Especially when I'm the visitor in their territory.

'Not to worry,' Anthon opened Henry's back door. 'You'll be completely safe in the tent. An elephant regards a tent as a solid item. If we don't bother them they won't bother us.'

We decided to camp right there, under the large Ana tree. First spreading out the groundsheet on the flattest part, we positioned and opened up the tent. Sleeping with your head downhill isn't a comfortable experience. Anthon returned to Henry and started to unpack the rest of our gear, clearly searching for something.

'Where did you put the tent poles, *Mein Schatz*?'

'I don't remember packing them,' I answered. 'Weren't they at your house?'

'I thought I last left them in your garage.' Anthon frowned.

'Oh my God! Titus hadn't packed them! How are we going to put the tent up without tent poles? We can't sleep in the open, not with the elephants around. And there are lion in the Ugab as well.' Once triggered, I've got an astounding ability to conjure worst-case scenarios.

'It's simple,' Anthon said, unperturbed by my agitation, 'we'll sleep on Henry's roof.'

I glanced up at the steel frame fitted on top of the vehicle. Three sides had restraining bars, the fourth was left unbarred, to allow a rooftop tent to open. How I regretted the absence of that tent at that moment.

'I'm going to roll down during the night. I move around a lot in my sleep.'

'I'll sleep that side,' Anthon replied, following my gaze.

'But what about the *erephants*?' I continued, 'they're as high as Henry's roof, and a *rion* can easily jump on the bonnet.' Stress caused me to also start confusing my r's and l's.

By this time he was folding double with laughter.

'Okay, okay,' I decided negotiation might be a better option. 'Why don't I help you to take everything out of the Land Rover, then we can sleep inside?' I knew full well the seats couldn't fold down anymore, that we wouldn't be able to stretch out, that we'd have a horrible night.

'*Mein Schatz,*' Anthon grabbed me by the arm, still laughing, trying to get me to look him in the eyes, 'it'll be as safe as sleeping in a tent. Trust me!'

'Can we at least park Henry next to that *koppie*?' I pointed to a nearby hillock of huge granite boulders. 'Then we can hop onto it when the elephants come.' I remembered hearing somewhere elephants have difficulty climbing over rocks.

'Well, it's not a bad idea; not for the midnight mountaineering bit, but for the prime stargazing we'll be able to do.' He ruffled his hand through my hair, still roaring with laughter.

I stirred from my daydream.

'Heloooo! I'm talking to you!' Anthon's voice reached me from afar, so engrossed was I in my own recollection, a bit delirious from the heat.

I shook myself awake and turned around in my seat to take a bottle of cold water from the Engel, which is always standing behind me. I took a sip and handed the bottle to him.

'We just drove past a Mopane which must've been torn apart by an elephant this morning. The branches were still fresh,' he gulped down half the water in the bottle.

'Oh yes, the elephants,' I returned to the straw coloured landscape, Henry's humming engine and the heat.

'You were right about the stargazing,' I said, 'that night we slept on top of Henry. It was spectacular.'

'Was a good idea of mine, wasn't it?' He brushed his fingers over my cheek. 'Although both of us had trouble sleeping. You had strange dreams and I refused to go into a deep sleep as I worried about you rolling over the edge.'

'I dreamt of elephants the entire night,' I defended my tossing and turning.'They were sniffing my hair. They were slithering their long rubbery trunks under our sleeping bags, curling them around us, picking us up and swinging us far into the Milky Way.'

'Do you remember how damp the outsides of our sleeping bags were when the chirping of the birds woke us the next morning at dawn?'

'I do. The only light was a drizzle of orange in the east. Soon after we heard the bees buzzing louder and louder,' I added.

'We looked at each other and without a word jumped to the ground, grabbing the mattress, the sleeping bags and the pillows, chucking everything into Henry. We fled out of the valley, not waiting for the bees to figure out that our damp sleeping bags might be a miraculous new water source,' Anthon completed the saga, smiling at me.

'But the highlight was stopping on the edge of the

escarpment, from where we could see the sunrise over the sleeping Ugab River Valley.'

'And I brewed you another perfect cup of coffee.' He gave a deep sigh. 'You're right. I'm a master at finding excuses for camping trips. Perfect camping trips.'

We hadn't seen any further signs of elephants. I sunk low in my seat and surrendered to the sleep which had been causing a fuzziness behind my eyes for some time.

Chapter 15

AS THE MOON SETS, SO THE SUN RISES

'We'll be leaving Kaokoland and entering Damaraland soon.' Anthon woke me from my uncomfortable head-rolling half-slumber, induced by the hour after midday and Henry's humming lullaby. When I'd finally cleared my head, I couldn't see the road.

I focused on our swinging Makalani trinket, then on Henry's chipped and splattered windscreen. Beyond that our second spare tyre rattled on the bonnet, against a backdrop of dust and blue.

I sat up straight. In front of us, the track plunged into the valley. Ridge upon ridge dematerialised into dusty blue. Far away a series of grey-green specks shivered, betraying the position of a watercourse.

'The Hoanib River Valley,' Anthon answered my unspoken question. 'We'll pass Fort Sesfontein soon. The German *Schutztruppe* built an outpost here just before the end of the nineteenth century.'

'Been there!' I bragged, now wide awake.

'I recall you mentioning something about that. Was in the mid-eighties, not so?'

'Yep. Varsity friends took us on a trip through Damaraland. The furthest north one could go without a permit in those days was Palmwag. From there we bought a day pass to travel to Fort Sesfontein. It was September; the time of year when the east wind churns up enough dust to make the sun disappear at four in the afternoon.'

Descending into the valley, the road passed through a rugged landscape looking as if a prehistoric mole of monstrous proportions had been pushing up from underneath, fragmenting and cracking the brittle layer of rock above. A swatch of magenta clashed wildly with its dusty surroundings.

'Stop!' I cried, 'I want to see what that is.'

'There are more further down the hill,' Anthon now also took notice. 'Looks like flowers. How strange, they seem to be growing out of the rocks.'

Candelabras of gorgeous lilies squeezed their stalks and buds through the cracks between the rocks, above which they hovered like suspended pink butterflies. Perhaps they suspected it was going to be a wet summer. As yet no rain had fallen this far south in Kaokoland.

The Hoanib River also showed signs of having flooded recently, pools of water still visible here and there. My gaze was drawn to the monumental mountains guarding the valley. Bare jagged rocks rose steeply from the flood plain, resembling a giant caramel *torte* of innumerable wafer-thin layers, squashed up and sliced at an angle with a sharp knife.

'To the trained eye, these mountains must be a geological history book going back millions of years,' Anthon said with admiration, 'a bit like the year rings of a tree.'

'My dad would've loved a trip like this,' I articulated a thought I'd often entertained during the last two days. 'He would've been able to explain to us how these mountains were formed; how old they were.'

'I thought he was a medical doctor?'

'Another lengthy story,' I laughed. 'He was quite a remarkable man. Always dreamed of becoming a doctor, but there was no money for him to study. He took a long detour to get there.'

'Fill me in?'

'His story isn't glamorous, my dear; not one of wealth, massive farms and illustrious forefathers with long names, like yours.'

I wondered where the appropriate place would be to begin with the story of a life.

From the corner of my eye, I noticed Anthon glancing at me fleetingly, before looking at the road again. 'As you should know by now, glamour and riches don't guarantee a good ending,' he said.

But we'll get to that part of the story as well. When he's ready.

'My father was born with another surname,' I decided to start right at the beginning.

'The youngest of six children, he was a baby when his parents died in some sort of an accident.' I always find it difficult to tell a story when 'facts' have decayed and withered with time. Like an old silk scarf, frayed and eaten by moths, leaving the completion of patterns to one's own imagination.

'According to my mother, he was hardly six months old. My brother remembers him mentioning two years. I assumed it was a motor car accident, my brother recalls a more sinister version. Whatever the truth, he was orphaned very young. Yet, he was the lucky one of the siblings.'

'Why do you say that?' Anthon asked.

'A childless couple adopted him. The older boys had to go and work to stay alive. I've got no idea what became of them. If they took up contact with my dad, I never knew about it.'

'When did this take place?'

'Four or five years after the First World War. People were poor.'

'And the others?'

'His sisters were placed with wealthy families as servants. One was more fortunate. She was placed with well-to-do apple farmers from the Ceres area. They treated her more like a daughter than a servant. Their son and heir fell in love with her, and she with him; later they were married and had a long and happy life together. She kept in touch with my father. His adopted parents didn't want him to know he wasn't their own son, so he was told the kind lady who visited him so often was a friend of the family. They only told him the truth when he was sixteen. He was furious that they had 'lied' to him. He never completely forgave them for not telling him sooner. His stepfather died before my father's twentieth birthday. He retained his birth surname as a second name, but decided to keep his adopted surname.'

'Where did he grow up?' Anthon asked.

'Franschhoek. His stepfather worked for the South African Railways, his stepmother was a teacher. Although he did well at school, his parents didn't see the need for further education. He told me they couldn't afford it. On completion of his schooling, at the end of 1940, he enlisted in the South African Air Force, trained as a radio operator and was sent to North Africa. Taken prisoner by the Germans at Tobruk, he ended the war as a POW in Italy. After his return home, he'd made enough money to enrol at Stellenbosch University for a B.Sc in Chemistry and Geology. That's where he met my mother.'

'So he followed the same route I did, first a B.Sc, then Medicine?' Anthon asked.

'Not quite. His path was much longer. He first needed to make enough money to pay for his further studies. With his degree, he landed a job in the chemistry and metallurgical lab of a gold mine near Jo'burg, where my mother joined him after she'd graduated as a dietician. But yes, he still wanted to study medicine. When he heard Stellenbosch University was launching an MB.Ch.B. degree in 1956, he enrolled and was part of the first intake of medical students to qualify there. He was 32 years old when he started his medical degree.'

'So that's why you grew up in Stellenbosch,' Anthon interrupted.

'I nearly didn't,' I laughed.

'Why?'

'After his housemanship year, my dad worked as a medical officer at the State Pathologist in Cape Town. His work and research focused on improving the smallpox and rabies vaccinations. When I was around six, he was awarded a year-long scholarship to further his studies in virology, in Toronto, Canada. My mother refused to accompany him. Her excuse was that she had three small children at home. Yet, at roughly the same time, her sister had no problem accompanying her husband to Holland with four children of which the youngest was a baby.'

'Reminds me of my mother,' he replied dryly.

'I'm not criticising her,' I tried to defend my mom, whom I loved dearly, 'but a year away from your dad when you're that young creates a distance which isn't easy to bridge later on in life.'

'Anyway, when my dad came back, he wasn't only in love with Canada, but also realised the country offered opportunities which South Africa couldn't compete with at the time; financially as well as regarding the political situation. He was all fired up to go and work in Canada. My mom refused point blank. It was too far away from her family, she said.'

'And again, our stories ran along parallel lines,' he murmured.

I nodded. 'I've often wondered how different our family's lives would've been, had we emigrated to Canada. Then again, I wouldn't have met you.'

My attention shifted. We reached a settlement of mud

brick structures scattered between tall date palms. Their green fronds appeared exotic and out of place in contrast to the landscapes we'd passed through earlier.

'Are there really six fountains here?' I asked.

'There are several fountains in the area. I assume there must be six, otherwise it wouldn't be called Sesfontein,' he chuckled. 'The German soldiers planted a number of palms around the fort. As you can see, they'd flourished during the last hundred years.'

'It does have the feel of an oasis,' I agreed.

We passed a series of homemade sign boards spaced just far enough apart to make sure their message was reinforced. The large squiggly characters appeared to have been written by one of the children.

'TIRE REPAIR,' I read, both capital r's facing in the wrong direction. 'I wonder if they can repair you when you're tired,' I joked.

'A colleague of mine told me they've got a rather ingenious method of acquiring customers for their tyre repair shops in this part of the world,' Anthon chuckled. 'When business is a bit slow, the kids are reputedly sent to place a few small planks, with nails sticking upwards, in the road.'

'Do you believe it's true?' I started scanning the road ahead for suspicious sharp objects. Having to change a flat tyre in this heat isn't my idea of fun.

'It might've happened, but I don't believe anybody needs to puncture tyres on purpose to get business in these parts. Damaraland is known for its rocky roads. If you want to curse someone in Namibia, you tell them you hope they'll come back in their next life as a tyre in Damaraland.'

We passed a small shed in the shade of a tree, a large sign above the open shopfront painted with TIRE REPAIR SHOP, again with the r's facing in the wrong direction. For the next kilometre, the signs were planted on the opposite side of the road and facing the oncoming traffic. At least they had a well-developed marketing strategy.

'Talking of punctures!' Anthon exclaimed as we passed a stationary minibus. I tried to make sense of the writing on its side, underneath a thick layer of dust. Pictures of the Big Five was the giveaway. Its occupants spilled into the road, clicking away at anything and everything. Two men were in the process of jacking up the car, the back right tyre in shreds.

Anthon slowed down, then reversed until he was opposite them.

'Need any help?' he asked. In these parts, it's good manners to stop and offer assistance when you pass a fellow traveller in distress. You never know when it'll be your turn.

'We're fine,' one of the two replied, without looking up. Then the other one, a portly gentleman with grey hair and beard, shouted, 'Doc Anthon! What're you doing here?'

'Smitty Klein!' A huge grin spread over Anthon's face. 'Since when are you guiding for Wild Nam Safari's?'

'A man must do what a man must do,' he beamed. 'I couldn't just sit at home. The missus drove me crazy.' By now the driver had also turned around to greet us.

'Need help?' Anthon asked.

'All under control,' Smitty smiled. 'Where are you heading, Doc?'

'Palmwag,' Anthon answered.

'In that case, there's one thing you can do for us,' Smitty switched to Afrikaans, not wanting his clients to understand what he was about to ask. *'Het julle tog nie vir ons 'n koue biertjie nie? Sal dit weer vir julle teruggee in Palmwag.'* ('Have you got a cold beer for us? Will return it to you at Palmwag.')

Anthon obliged with two beers and a smile. As we pulled away he said, 'that's why I never undertake a trip in these parts without at least two spare tyres. Of course, an extra six-pack of beer will never go unused either.'

'This country is so vast, yet you always manage to bump into someone you know,' I shook my head in disbelief.

'Smitty is a patient of mine. Been a tour guide for as long as I've known him. A year ago he made an appointment to see me, asking for my advice. His wife wanted him to retire. I suggested giving it a go, but I knew he'd crack up sitting at home.'

'I've told you often, retirement is the single biggest cause of early death,' I agreed. 'We're doing something right with these trips; working less and enjoying more.'

'Some people are of the opinion we hid a pot of gold somewhere, that's why we can 'afford' to do this,' he added.

'But we did! We figured out when enough is enough,' I laughed, but I was deadly serious.

We'd been driving in a wide valley thick with Mopane shrub.

'I recognise this road,' I said, 'but previously we didn't continue into the Kaokoveld.'

'You're right,' Anthon confirmed. 'See that turnoff, where the road takes a curve to the right? That's the road to Ongongo. We camped there last year in September.'

'When you woke me before the sun was up, to see the moon setting as the sun was rising?' One of my special recollections. One with photographs.

Ongongo is also known by its German name, *Warmquelle,* meaning a spring of warm water. As its name implies, it's another oasis in this arid region; a pool of lukewarm opalescent water, filled by a perennial waterfall. This, in turn, is fed by a rivulet originating from the source itself. I know, as we went in search of it on that September morning.

Anthon woke me before dawn. I was in no mood to leave the warmth of our down duvet.

'It's not even light,' I complained, 'why do you want me to get dressed and climb up the hill?'

He just laughed and handed me my clothes. 'You won't regret it,' he promised.

Still half asleep I crawled out of the tent, the cool of morning biting my bare legs. I stumbled after him without enthusiasm. When we reached the top of the escarpment, the full moon hovered above the hollow between two mountains. I gasped, my lethargy was forgotten. We sat down on a rock. He pulled me close, wrapping his jacket around my body. We were alone on earth, the blue half-light between day and night painting the veldt with a sorcerer's brush, while the moon, like a giant pearl, drifted into its sinuous cradle below. As the last slither dropped away, the crests of the mountains burst into flames.

'Turn around,' Anthon whispered.

Behind us, the sun emerged above the opposite hills.

We were suspended between night and day.

I could feel my entire body filling with energy, renewed by sharing in this moment of Gaia's breathing. I jumped up and held out my hand to my still seated partner.

'Now that I'm finally wide awake, let's find the source,' I shouted while trying to pull him up.

'The source?' Anthon's expression exclaimed that I was the crazy one. His thoughts were still lingering in the serenity between the setting moon and the rising sun.

'The eye of the fountain, of course!' I felt like hopping over rocks, slurping up the last cool of the night which still clung to the grass. 'Come on Doc, soon we'll be clobbered by the heat again.'

The Ongongo rock pool hides in a gorge, so insignificant it can be called a gulley, carved by aeons of water trickling into it. The camping area is squeezed into this ravine, an oasis of giant ficus trees. The surrounding escarpment is a different world. Still encircled by mountains, the river feeding the waterfall is wide and empty, a small trickle of water collecting here and there between the smooth river rocks.

'The fountain must be over there,' Anthon pointed to a colossal ficus tree, its gnarled roots snaking into the river, looking like a Medusa's head of writhing boa constrictors.

Leaping from rock to rock, I reached it first. 'Nope,' I shouted, 'it must be further up.'

'Well, just follow the water,' Anthon joked.

Not far from the ficus, we stumbled upon a deep pool of water, hidden by its craggy rim. A mirror of liquid silver.

'This must be one of Phillip Pullman's doorways to another universe,' I leaned over a boulder, touching the water with my hand. Concentric circles pulled and twisted the upside down landscape around my finger.

'Or perhaps it's a Dali painting,' I changed my mind.

'I think it's something far more useful, especially early in the morning when there's no shower available,' was Anthon's comment from the far side of the pool.

Hunched over the water gurgling from the earth, he was splashing his face.

From my vantage point, droplets of crystal dangled in time, suspended on beams of early-morning sun.

I felt something touching my knee.

'Wake up, Mein Schatz, or you'll miss your first glimpse of Damaraland.' Anthon was shaking my leg to wake me from my daydream.

I obliged. I was slipping away once again. I wanted to stay awake and enjoy the drama of this landscape.

'It looks as if it had rained here during the last week or so,' he commented.

A silky brush of lime lingered over the earth. The road rose and fell with the landscape, each rise revealing a fresh vista. Wave upon wave of hills, strewn with red rocks, disappeared into the distance. Flat-topped mountains provided the backdrop.

'Grey-green Euphorbias, fleshy white bottle trees, purple hills; what a contrast,' I'm smitten with the colours and shapes of Damaraland.

Bottle trees are bizarre. Bulbous trunks are topped with spindly necks from which one or two thorn-covered branches clutched into space. They might have sprouted from the imagination of Dr Seuss.

'There's one close to the road, not too far from here,' Anthon read my mind. 'We can stop there and have a look.'

'And a beer. And a smoke,' he added.

Rounding a corner, the phantom tree loomed large right next to Henry. Anthon grabbed a beer, ice cold from the Engel, for us to share. Squeezing into the plant's scraggly shade, we attempted to restore liquid to our bodies. Up close its bark was smooth and grey-white, dented and scarred by age. I could swear I heard it sigh. A benign, comical creature, only its toes, firmly entangled between the smooth round red rocks, prevented it from wobbling down the hill and disappearing into a fairytale.

'Last year they were full of white flowers,' I remembered, 'but we had to push through to Windhoek and had no time to stop.'

At this Anthon looked at his watch. 'Thanks for reminding me. We need to get going.'

I reluctantly left the ancient creature to return to the secret life it lived when human eyes were averted.

Chapter 16

RED PLUMS AND MORE ELEPHANT DUNG

'There must be a donkey cart ahead,' Anthon pointed at the spoor of a two-wheeled cart. It swayed to and fro through the dust as the driver tried to guide the donkeys away from the worst rocks and dips.

'From where, to where?' I wondered.

We'd travelled at least 60km since leaving Sesfontein.

During that time a number of tiny Damara settlements came and went. These usually comprised a large area cleared of all the smaller trees. A few dwellings built of mud bricks and corrugated iron were scattered between the remaining larger Mopane trees and the ubiquitous carpet of red rocks. Goats clustered together in the shade, sometimes climbing on top of each other to escape the heat of the sun or to reach a green Mopane leaf.

The first sign of a village is the spindly steel structure of the windmill guarding a borehole, pumping precious water from deep under the surface of the desert into a corrugated iron or concrete dam. I noticed that in most villages a wide rim of large stones surrounded these structures.

'Is it true that elephants can't walk over rocks?' I've been meaning to ask Anthon this for some time, but it always slipped my mind.

'When closely packed, they've got great difficulty walking over it,' he answered.

'So the rocks which the villagers arrange around the water points do have a purpose?'

'For sure,' he replied, 'when left unprotected, a thirsty elephant will crunch a windmill into a heap of scrap metal in no time. We'll soon pass through a village where this had happened not too long ago.'

Not two kilometres further he slowed down, pointing at the tangled remains of a triangulated steel structure and a crumpled mass of corrugated iron sheeting.

'Looks like a squashed beer can,' I commented.

'A large elephant is strong enough to do that to a dam full of water,' Anthon said. 'Can you imagine how much damage a small herd can do?'

'No wonder the villagers aren't as fond of them as we are,' I observed.

The cart tracks were still snaking across the road, showing us the way.

'There's a Damara family living over the next hill,' Anthon said. 'They've got a curio stall by the roadside. It could be their donkey cart we're following.'

'Oh yes! The one selling elephant dung and crystals,' I recalled.

'That's it,' he replied. 'Shall we stop and see what they've got today?'

'Of course!' was my obvious answer.

Soon after a rickety structure of driftwood and grass appeared ahead. As we drew closer, I could make out a handwritten sign: 'Stop 'n Shop 4 U,' it read; 'Welcome to Namibia,' said the other side. Crystals and rocks were displayed on makeshift shelves; mobiles of dried elephant dung, gnarled pieces of wood and thorny seeds hung from a dead tree branch planted upright for that purpose.

'Where's the shopkeeper?' I asked.

'Don't you worry, he'll soon pitch up,' Anthon explained. 'See that stone hut in the distance? That's where the family lives. They already know about us. They're just waiting to see whether we stop and get out of the car before they come down here.'

'Makes sense in this heat,' I agreed.

We parked Henry in front of the stall. As Anthon opened his door, a man came out of the house, followed by a child in a yellow and red dress.

He waved at them.

I took a photo of him posing under the 'Welcome to Namibia' sign. One needs a tourist shot every now and then.

I inspected the rocks and crystals, picking out the ones I preferred and stashing them to one side. Anthon was intrigued by the elephant-dung mobile.

'I think this will be an excellent addition to our stoep,' he grinned.

I gave him a questioning look. 'Why?'

'I believe this to be the Damara version of a dream catcher,' he answered. 'Perhaps it will act as a poo-catcher.'

'What do you mean? Why do you want to catch poo on our stoep?'

'It might ensnare all the shit sent our way by the soon-to-be-previous Missus,' he emphasised the 'snare' bit and rolled his eyes, as he hooked the mobile from the branch and added it to my pile.

By now the man and the little girl had joined us.

'*Mi-re*!' Anthon greeted him in Damara. A wide grin crinkled his face. '*Mi-re*!' he returned the greeting, holding out his hand. Two wide eyes observed us from behind his legs.

'*Het dit al kom reën?*' ('Has the rain come yet?'), Anthon asked him in Afrikaans as he shook his hand.

'*Nee Meneer, nog niks nie,*' (Not yet, Mister, not yet.') He shook his head, replying in the same language, '*ons het vir vier jaar nog nie reën gesien nie.*' ('We hadn't seen any rain for four years.')

'You might be lucky soon,' Anthon consoled him, 'lots of rain to the east.'

'What's the elephant dung for?' Anthon asked, pointing at a pile of dried chunks of dung, the large percentage of straw giving away its origin.

'It's excellent for keeping the Mopane flies away,' the man answered. 'When you camp and you're bothered by them, you pack the dung balls out around your camp. You then put a small piece of burning coal on top of each piece. The smoke will chase the flies away.'

'Interesting,' Anthon said. 'Perhaps we should try it next time.'

Then he pointed at my pile of rocks and crystals.

'How much?' he asked.

'If you've got some rice or beans or potatoes?' the man paused, looking at us expectantly. He'd noticed we were campers.

'You see, Mister, if you pay with money,' he wrung his hands, his eyes scanning the veldt as if he was considering the best way to explain his predicament, 'I've got to go to Sesfontein to buy food for my family.' He returned his gaze to hold Anthon's. 'It takes me a day to get there with my donkey cart and a day to come back again. That's why it's better for me if you pay with food or clothing.' Then, glancing furtively towards the house, where a thin old woman was coming out of the door, he added: 'I also have a problem with my *Ousie – my* wife —, she likes to drink too much. If you pay with money she wants to buy Drink.'

I looked at Anthon. 'We've only got one night of camping left,' I said to him. 'Let's see what we can spare.'

I found two tins of tomatoes and a box of pasta, our emergency provisions had our road been blocked by a river in flood. A small packet of sugar and a full bag of maize meal joined the pile.

'Keep two potatoes for tonight, then he can have the rest as well,' Anthon added. The man looked well pleased with the trade. The little girl emerged from behind his legs. No more than four years old, she held out both her hands. 'Sweets?' she whispered, her brown eyes large with expectation.

I shook my head. We don't eat much by way of sweets and if we did, I prefer not to give them to these kids. Then I remembered something better. Opening the Engel I took out a few apples and a bright red plum. I gave the apples to the man and held out the plum towards the child. Her face showed no sign of recognition. She'd obviously never seen anything like it before. Even her father eyed the fruit with distrust.

'Take a bite,' I coaxed, crouching down to her level, my camera at the ready. She looked at her father for approval. He nodded and said something in Damara. She looked back at me, touching the plum with her finger. The temptation of tasting the ice cold, berry-red fruit, was too big. Without breaking eye contact with me, her small hand closed around it and brought it to her mouth. She bit into the plum, juice trickling onto her chin. Wonder spread over her face as the acidic sweetness touched her tongue. Holding it some distance away, she inspected it, then brought it closer and licked the fruit again. We were forgotten as she and her plum entered that childhood world where everything was still possible.

I stood up. The man's wife had now joined us. Emaciated, leathery, toothless, she appeared ancient. Yet, looking at him, I realised she was much younger than I was. The contrast between the child and her mother couldn't have been greater: the one filled with unlimited potential, the other, her body ravaged by alcohol, empty of promise.

It was time to leave. With a final Damara greeting, we climbed back into Henry.

As he turned the key and Henry's engine chugged to life, Anthon looked at me, his eyes thoughtful. 'Do you realise if it hadn't rained here for four years, that kid had never experienced rain before either?'

From here the road wound upwards until we crested the next hill and one of my favourite panoramas rolled out over Henry's bonnet.

'The Etendeka Plateau,' Anthon confirmed. 'Did you know it's a Himba word meaning The Place of the Flat-topped Mountains?'

'Makes sense,' I agreed, entranced by the landscape. The gravel road folded over the rust-brown hills and into the valleys, forming a series of diminishing trapeziums cut out of sandpaper, one stacked upon the other, wide edge ever to the bottom. The lowering sun drew a long black shadow trailing each tree and rock. Faraway the warm ochre hues crashed into a wall of purple-blue mountains; drawn in elegant wide brush strokes, as if by the playful hand of a painter.

'This is what I visualise when I hear the name Damaraland,' I said. Henry's song dropped an octave as Anthon geared down to first. We slipped into the valley.

'I think I'll make up a story about a pre-historic tribe who picked these rocks by hand, then, with great precision, packed them one next to the other, until the entire plateau was covered in red stone,' I continued. 'They all seem to be the same shape, size and colour.'

'You can add a celestial gardener who planted the thousands of spiky grey-green Euphorbias in between,' he added.

'How do the elephants manage to walk here?' I asked, remembering the wind pumps in the Damara villages we drove through.

'The rocks aren't quite as close together as it might seem

from the car,' he answered. 'In most places, an elephant can easily navigate a path between them. Of course, if there's a road they'll take the easier route.'

'That explains the tracks in the gravel we see so often.'

'See those trails meandering down the slope?' he pointed to a series of narrow tracks converging at a clump of trees in the bottom of the valley. 'They're game paths. I assume there's a water source under those Acacias.'

As if to prove his point, a number of springbok appeared from the shade. One behind the other, they strolled up the hillside.

We reached the top of the next hill. To our left, glowing like striped copper in the evening sun, a herd of zebra blended into the side of the mountain. On hearing the approaching vehicle, they lifted their heads, stopped chewing and stared at us. As if to say, 'only another couple of tourists', the large stallion jerked his head to the side, snorted and led his harem further up the mountain.

'They're lovely,' I remarked. 'Is it the sun or are they much browner than usual? Their white stripes appear to take on the hue of the red-brown landscape.'

'They're Hartman's Zebra,' Anthon explained. 'Look at their legs: their stripes continue right down to their feet. One of the local guides told me you recognise them by their striped socks. And yes, sometimes they tend to be more reddish-brown than the common type.'

'We should be at Palmwag before the sun goes down,' Anthon read my mind. 'We're in for a spectacle. See those tall palm trees ahead? Your next kitsch African sunset and an ice cold gin and tonic are awaiting you.'

Soon after we arrived at the lodge.

'They've rebuilt it completely,' I remarked. 'I still

remember it as consisting of a couple of reed huts with thatched roofs. Palmwag used to be the last outpost before the war zone; and yes, I do remember the flamboyant sunsets of tall Makalani palms against a blazing orange sky.'

'Well, let's try and catch the sundown then,' Anthon hurried me up. 'We're now back in civilisation. We can set-up camp after dark. They've got lights at the campsites.'

Parking Henry at the entrance, we booked ourselves in. Then we hurried along the meandering pathway, down to the reed bed where the Uniab River creates the Palmwag oasis. As we reached the bar area, the sun collected its last rays and dropped from sight. A group of tourists flashed away at the spectacle as if a burst of light from a camera would catch the dying sun. Not bothered by either the tourists or missing the sunset, Anthon aimed directly for the bar and ordered a beer and a gin and tonic. Then he flopped down on the nearest lounger.

'This is the life!' he exclaimed, wiping the foam from his upper lip. Gin and tonic in hand, I felt disturbed and irritated by the presence of the khaki-clad crowd. Our few days of solitude left me unprepared for sharing my space with other humans. They seemed to be all around me, cluttering the view, babbling like noisy chickens, reminding me of the rush we'd be returning to the next day.

'Calm down, *Mein Schatz*,' Anthon grabbed me by the hand and pulled me down next to him. 'Cheers!' his beer bottle touched my glass. 'To another amazing detour.'

I forced myself back to the present, realising all was well as long as we were together.

'Cheers!' I agreed. Sinking back into the crook of his arm, I sipped my icy drink, soothed by the whisper of palm leaves swaying in the cool westerly breeze.

Chapter 17

OF LAUGHING HYENAS AND A PINK G-STRING

'Doc Anthon!' The silhouette approaching against the still incandescent sky had a familiar voice and profile.

'Identify yourself!' Anthon answered, his free arm hooked over the back of the bench, his legs stretched out in front of him. 'I'm too tired to get up.'

'Wow, Rob, what're you doing here?' My brain was first to match the voice and outline to someone familiar.

'For an architect, you can ask some stupid questions, *Mein Schatz,*' Anthon laughed, now also recognising the person in front of us. 'He's a tour guide. They tend to lurk around places like these.'

I pulled myself up to give our friend a hug. 'Are those your charges?' I pointed at a noisy group on their way to the dining area.

Rob laughed. 'No, luckily I'm not guiding at the moment. Your question wasn't all that stupid after all,' he answered. 'Elfriede and I are running a lodge not too far from here. I came to Palmwag to fetch a couple of guests with car trouble. Seems the problem isn't as easy to fix as I thought, so I'll have to stay the night. But what're you two doing here? Haven't you got work to do, like normal people?'

Anthon chuckled as he held out his hand. 'We're on our way back from work, I guess.'

'We just took the scenic route home,' I added.

'Thought it was your Defender I saw in the parking lot,' Rob replied. 'Camping or staying in the lodge?'

'Camping,' Anthon answered.

'Good,' Rob said. 'Mind if I come by for a drink after dinner? Have to join my guests for supper tonight.'

'Great,' Anthon replied. 'We still have to set up camp. Should have a fire ready by the time you're done here.'

As we finished our drinks, we watched Rob join a middle-aged couple at their dinner table.

'They look nice enough,' I commented, 'at least they're not dressed like Dr Livingstone and his troupe.'

Another familiar figure appeared out of the darkness, waving two bottles of beer at us.

'Repayment of my debt, as promised,' Smitty Klein grinned.

'So the group of cackling ducks belong to you?' Anthon joked.

'I'm their honourable leader.' He bowed deeply in front of us, handing Anthon the two beers. '*Aag*, they're a sweet bunch,' he defended his herd, 'and completely in love with Namibia.'

'Then I'm prepared to forgive them for being such loyal safari shop customers,' I mocked.

By the time we'd finished our drinks and swapped a bit of gossip with Smitty, night had fallen. Setting up camp in the dark is a pain, even if the campsite has an electric light. At this stage of the trip, Henry's interior looked like a messy teenager's room. We decided to open the rooftop tent, where the bedding was already stored, pack out the chairs and table and start the fire.

'Do you know what?' I muttered to myself, 'this mess can be sorted out when we arrive back in Windhoek.'

'I agree,' Anthon chirped from where he was setting up the table, then added, '*Schatzie*, please hand me the lighter?'

'Where do I find it?' I asked, not in the mood to search without a plan.

'In the glove compartment?' he took a chance.

'Nope, not there,' I revealed after scratching in the box between the seats, in the dark.

'Try and find the pants I wore last night,' he considered option two.

'Which is somewhere in the chaos on the back seat,' I confirmed.

'Have you tried putting your hand in your pocket?' I

suggested. 'You always seem to find a lighter there when you want to smoke a cigarette?'

'*Scheiße*!' he swore in German, 'I must've left it where we had our drinks.'

At that moment he opened Henry's left back door to get to the Engel. A shoe and the elephant-dung mobile tumbled out.

'It seems as if Henry is screaming at us to tidy him up,' I laughed, resigned to the necessity of the task before we could light our fire.

'I'll help you,' Anthon offered. The task took no more than a couple of minutes. Just as well we did it, as we also found a banana entering an advanced stage of decay, as well as our torch, a much-needed piece of camping equipment, especially for those with small bladders. Here the lodge generator was still switched off at ten sharp in the evening.

Rob joined us halfway through our meal. A jovial, handsome man in his early forties, he was one of the most accomplished tour guides in Namibia. His knowledge of all things Namibian, nature-related of course, was encyclopaedic. Thinking ahead, he brought a folding chair from the lodge, which he set up next to the fire. He declined to join us for a bite but accepted a glass of red wine.

'I'm afraid you'll have to settle for the stainless steel cup. We only have two glasses,' I apologised as I handed him the wine.

Rob just laughed. 'Cheers guys, good to be here with you. Please carry on with your meal.'

I unfolded my jacket potato from its foil wrapping and cut it open to cool before returning to my plate of succulent lamb chops, still slightly pink on the inside, the thin rim of fat crisped to perfection.

'Nice wine!' Rob said with appreciation.

'Life's to short to drink *kak* wine,' Anthon quipped.

'Special friends and special places call for special wine,' I added.

'Yes, Damaraland is a magical place,' Rob agreed. 'Did you bump into the resident elephant?'

'No,' I answered, dropping a chunk of butter onto my potato. 'Haven't seen any ellies on this entire trip.'

'We've only seen elephant tracks so far,' Anthon lamented. 'We're starting to believe the Existence of the Desert Elephant is a conspiracy theory.' Sitting with a lamb chop in one hand, Anthon tried to wipe his mouth with the back of the other, spreading a layer of fat over his cheek; as happy as a toddler with an ice cream.

'He often wanders around the reed bed in the river,' Rob elaborated. 'Sometimes the entire herd passes through here. You might hear him moving through the reeds before you see him. He's docile, though. Doesn't bother with the campers.'

'Had any interesting encounters with wildlife since we last saw you?' Anthon asked as he tried to clean his face and hands with the piece of paper towel I handed him.

'I think we'll only get you clean under a shower,' I laughed, as he only managed to spread the mess further.

'Mmmm,' Rob took the cue. 'Talking of showers, we'd had quite an interesting experience when Elfriede and I went camping in Botswana last year.' He took a sip of wine. 'We arrived at the deserted campsite late afternoon, pitched our tent, then decided to go for a shower before we started our fire. I scouted for animals as we set up camp, but all seemed clear. We took our towels and a bottle of shampoo and headed for the ablutions. One of those standard two-by-two-metre structures with a door on one side and an opening serving as a window on the other. It was fairly dark inside. We opened the tap and took turns to wet our hair, then shampooed ourselves. I had my eyes closed, so as not to get them full of soap, when the water suddenly stopped. I opened my eyes, but it was pitch dark. Elfriede grabbed my arm, put her hand over my mouth and pulled me to the far side of the cubicle.'

'Are you sure Elfriede will be okay with you telling us this story?' Anthon joked. 'It sounds kinky to me.'

'Haha,' Rob chuckled, 'it depends whether you regard and elephant trunk as kinky.'

'An elephant trunk?' I asked.

'Well,' Rob continued, 'as my eyes adapted to the darkness, I saw what appeared to be a huge grey rubber hosepipe locked onto the showerhead and from there running through the window.'

Rob sat back and took another gulp of wine, then both he and Anthon burst out laughing as they saw my mystified expression.

Anthon ruffled my hair as he pulled me close, while Rob explained. 'While we were showering, an elephant stuck his trunk through the window, latched onto the showerhead and started to fill his stomach with our water.'

'Oh my God!' I laughed, finally visualising what happened. 'What did you do?'

'We crouched in the corner furthest away from the window and waited until he'd drunk enough. Fortunately for us he then wandered off. By that time we were both cold and hungry and ready to rid ourselves of the shampoo in our hair,' Rob concluded.

We all enjoyed a good laugh.

Anthon asked Rob about the mechanical problem his guests had with their vehicle. I had no interest in what happened under any car's bonnet, so I slipped away to rinse the few items we used for dinner, whereafter I packed everything in Henry's boot. On my return the fire was burning high again, the three chairs now arranged around it.

'Shhh…' Anthon held up his hand, listening intently. 'Did you hear that? Sounded like a hyena.'

Rob nodded in agreement as we heard it again. 'The Palmwag concession still teems with game. Lion, leopard, cheetah, hyena, to name only a few of the predators.' He scratched his chin, staring into the darkness beyond us. An impish smile creased his face. 'Did I ever tell you about the habit hyenas have of sleeping against one's tent at night?'

I settled into my chair with satisfaction. If Rob was in storytelling mode, we were in for an entertaining evening.

'Go ahead,' I nudged.

Rob put his hand in his left trouser pocket and pulled out his pipe. From the other pocket, he hauled a small leather pouch filled with tobacco and proceeded to stuff it into the shiny wooden vessel resting in the palm of his hand. Anthon topped-up our glasses and lit his own cigarette before offering the lighter to our friend.

Smoke twirled white against the glow of the fire. The warm light picked out our faces against the darkness enveloping our surroundings.

The mood was right.

'In Botswana, hyenas have discovered they can warm themselves by lying against an unsuspecting camper's tent at night,' Rob began. 'I've been woken by the pong of rotten meat more than once. It seeps into your innards and your dreams. Worse than having cold water chucked over you when you're asleep.'

'Yuk!' I grunted. 'Sounds revolting. How do you get rid of the hyena?'

'I've developed a trick,' he continued, puffing the pipe into life.

'Once I've figured out where it was lying, I position myself right next to the place where it indents the side of the tent. I then pull up my legs, trying not to make a noise, and kick it with both legs, as hard as I can.'

'And that chases a hyena away?' I asked.

'It probably sends it flying through the air, laughing.' Anthon found his own joke hilarious.

'But won't he try to bite you through the tent?' I persisted.

'I've tried to convince her she'll be perfectly safe in a tent on the ground, even if there are lions around,' Anthon told Rob, a look of mock exasperation on his face.

'Don't worry, they'll go for him first,' Rob quipped, jabbing in Anthon's direction with his pipe. Then, turning in my direction, 'in all seriousness, a wild animal regards a human in a tent or on an open vehicle as part of something much larger than itself. That's why it won't attack you,' Rob confirmed what I already knew, but still have trouble believing.

'But yes, a hard kick should persuade a hyena to move off to a better spot.' He looked at us, mischief crinkling around his eyes. I realised the story was still developing.

'A couple of seasons ago, I took a group of Americans on a self-drive camping safari through Botswana. If I remember correctly, the group consisted of four couples in three vehicles. I drove the fourth vehicle. The camping areas in

Botswana aren't fenced and facilities are rudimentary. It still feels as if you're camping wild, especially if there are no other campers around. Lion and other animals often enter your camp at night. Ablutions are basic long drops, inclusive of the lovely aroma which comes with them.'

Anthon nodded in agreement. Unlike me, he'd camped in Botswana a number of times.

Rob folded his right leg over the left, leaned slightly forward and balanced his elbow on his knee, cupping his pipe in his hand. While he puffed on it, his pensive expression gave away he was back in Botswana.

'When stopping for the night, we pulled the vehicles in a circle, far enough from the ablutions not to be bothered by the smell. The tents were put up fairly closely together, creating an open area around the fire where we could relax and share stories before we went to sleep. In Botswana, I always prohibit my clients from going to the toilet by themselves at night. If they really have to go, they know to call me. I don't mind walking with them. At least I know what to look out for and carry a firearm for their protection.'

'Makes sense,' I agreed.

'You can also pack a couple of plastic containers for that purpose?' Anthon joked.

'Some of my clients do exactly that,' Rob replied. 'On this specific evening, we all sat around the fire, drinking wine and telling lion stories. The one story more terrifying than the next, of course. It was getting late and I wanted us to start early the next morning, so I suggested it was time to turn in for the night. Part of the ritual was that I'd walk them to the ablutions and wait around, torch in my one hand and rifle in the other, until everybody had a chance to empty their bladders.'

'We were only two days into the trip and I didn't know my clients all that well yet. One couple concerned me a bit, though. Mel was an older man who drank quite a bit the first evening. His wife, Di, was a rather large, curvy blonde, much younger than him. She flirted with everybody. The more she teased, the more he seemed to drink.'

'Mmmm,' I smiled, 'and she probably didn't spare you either.'

Rob laughed. 'As a tour guide, I'm used to it. Comes with the job. I'd learnt how to nip it in the bud when I was quite young.'

Anthon burst out laughing. 'No pun intended, hey Rob?'

Rob chuckled, using the opportunity to pull on his pipe before resuming the yarn.

'Well, it was a warm evening and the missus decided to put on a tight little number which struggled to contain all of her. On top of that, she parked herself in between two of the other male guests, shivering with giggles every time either of them said anything remotely funny, all the while ignoring the hubby. He was quiet right through dinner and I took it for granted he was in a bad mood because of her antics. When I saw him fetching a full bottle of brandy, I thought it might be prudent to chase everybody to bed on the pretext of us needing to start early the next morning. I also suspected it was going to be a noisy night. Their tent was right next to mine. The previous night one of my guests snored like a tractor and I assumed it was him and his brandy.' Rob paused to take another deep draw.

By now our campfire was burning low. The moon hadn't risen yet, leaving centre stage to the Milky Way, exploding over us in a shower of brilliant superlatives. Anthon dropped another piece of wood on the coals, still pulsing red with a bit of life. Molten metal sparks challenged the glorious stars above.

Rob twirled the last bit of liquid in his cup, then resumed his tale.

'I made a point of walking all the ladies to the ablution block before bedtime.'

'Clever man,' Anthon laughed, as he poured us more wine.

'Finally all my guests were safely in their tents and with luck their bladders were empty,' Rob went on.

'I still wanted to do a bit of reading, so I lit a lantern, got undressed and crawled into my sleeping bag. With my legs pulled up, I balanced the book against my knees.' Rob imitated his position by resting both feet on the side of the brick pedestal on which our fire was now crackling again.

'The day had been long and I was tired. I dozed off while reading. I don't know how long I slept, but woke up when I felt something large falling back against the side of my tent, inches from my feet.' He indicated the distance with his pipe.

'"Freaking hyena!" I thought. In the background I could hear the American snoring. I was glad the hyena chose my tent and not theirs; I didn't feel like dealing with spooked clients that night. I decided to teach the animal a lesson.' Rob narrowed his eyes and switched to a whisper.

'Without making a sound, I pulled my legs up a bit further,' — he drew his feet closer to his bum —, 'then let go with full force, hoping to kick him hard enough to chase him into next year.' He kicked out his feet and gradually raised his voice. 'My feet connected with the indented weight on my tent. I could feel I got him full on the bum. I could just see the hyena flying through the air, then heard a thud as it hit the ground,' — he paused for a second, to further build up tension —, 'but instead of the expected yelp followed by the sound of running paws, I heard a high pitched female scream. "Oh shit!" I thought to myself, "I must've kicked the animal onto the Americans' tent!" I grabbed my flashlight in one hand and my gun in the other and rushed out of the tent, aiming the beam of light where I thought I'd heard the thud.'

Rob paused to take a deep draw from his pipe, both feet now back on the ground. He knew how to play his audience. Even Anthon was sitting with his cigarette in mid-air, eyes glued on Rob, not quite knowing what to expect.

'At first I couldn't comprehend what I was seeing,' — he paused again, his eyes fixed on the sputtering fire in front of him —, 'until I realised it was the illuminated naked nether parts of a rather large female, lying on her stomach, bum in the air and face in the sand, a pair of panties hooked around her ankles.'

Anthon gave a snort, indicating an explosion of laughter was building up in his stomach, but Rob pushed through, the glint in his eyes contradicting his dry tone.

'As it dawned on me I was staring at the bare bottom of Mel's flirty wife, he barged out of their tent, blinding me with the light from his own torch. And there I was, in my underpants, gun in the one hand, torch in the other, behind a blonde with her exposed backside gaping at me, a pink G-string knotted around her ankles, T-shirt bundled under her armpits. God alone knew what it must've looked like.'

By this time we could no longer contain ourselves. We were both screaming with laughter. Rob, a self-satisfied smirk around his mouth, sat with his pipe cupped in his hand, calmly persevering with this narrative.

'My automatic reaction was to lift my arms, which mercifully aimed the spotlight in another direction, while I shouted, "It's not what it looks like!" I expected Mel to at least take a swing at me.' Again he stared into the fire, a big smile spreading over his face for the first time since he commenced with the tale.

'Come on, Rob, what happened?' I urged.

He chuckled, 'Mel gave a roar of laughter. I expected the entire camp to be awake by now, but luckily no one stirred. Next, he grabbed a towel from their tent and covered up Di's backside while she struggled to untangle herself from her underwear. After helping her up, she disappeared inside, all her coquetry gone. I took the chance to pull a T-shirt over my head.'

He took the tobacco pouch from his pocket, knocked the last bit of ash from his pipe and began stuffing it again. Anthon and I were still wiping the tears from our eyes after our bout of hysterics.

'The night was warm and the full moon lit up the Savannah as if a giant spotlight was shining from above,' Rob continued.

'When Mel reappeared from his tent, he carried a bottle and two small stainless steel shot-glasses.' Rob lit the pipe, puffing a few times to get it going.

'Mel sat down on one of the camping chairs, indicating I must join him. I took a log of wood and rekindled the fire, sensing that like me, he was now far from sleepy. He poured each of us a nightcap.' Rob's pipe glowed red as he pulled on it deeply.

'Mel just sat there, softly chuckling to himself. "Come on, Mel," I pleaded, "talk to me." I mean, I still had no idea whether he suspected any hanky-panky while he was sleeping.'

'Hold your story,' Anthon interrupted. 'I now also feel like a cognac. Care to join me?' As Rob and I both nodded our approval, he fetched the bottle from Henry's drawer while I scratched in the crockery crate for shot-glasses. After another toast we were ready. Rob needed no encouragement to continue.

'Mel lifted his glass to me, unable to wipe the smile from his face. "Rob, I'm sorry, but it was just so funny," he started. Then he told me the whole story. Di wanted to go for a pee. He told her to wake me up, but she was too embarrassed. He noticed there was still a light on in my tent. Reckoning I'd be close enough to save the ol' lady, should a beast appear out of the night, he suggested she should squat in-between our tents. He'd keep watch. She pulled down her panties and lowered herself into a crouch. She must've lost her balance, because she stumbled backwards, against my tent. Next thing he saw his wife taking off like a rocket, her knickers knotting around her legs as she dove head first into the sand.'

Rob paused. His eyes danced in the firelight as he took a sip of cognac. 'I was a bit confused,' he resumed, 'I could swear I heard Mel snore earlier. "So you were awake all the time?" I asked him. "Of course I was!" he snorted, "how d'you expect me to sleep with half the camp grunting like pigs? I also had to be able to go and save the old girl should a lion develop the inclination to get a taste of her." Then he added, "it never really bugs me when she flirts like that. She's completely harmless. I love my Di just as she is."'

'That's so sweet,' I laughed.

'Was your trip not a bit awkward afterwards?' Anthon asked, 'you mentioned earlier Mel was a bit of grump?'

'Not at all,' Rob smiled. 'Mel and I became good friends. He told me he always suffers from jet lag for a good three days after a transatlantic flight. What I saw as a bad mood because of his wife, was him feeling under the weather. Once he'd adapted to the time zone and the climate, he was the mainstay of the group. We still have regular contact. He's talking about doing another safari in a year or two.'

'And the wife?' I was curious.

'Di?' he laughed, 'She stopped her shit and started to dress properly, especially after the sun and the mozzies got hold of her.'

Chapter 18

AGATES IN AIR BUBBLES

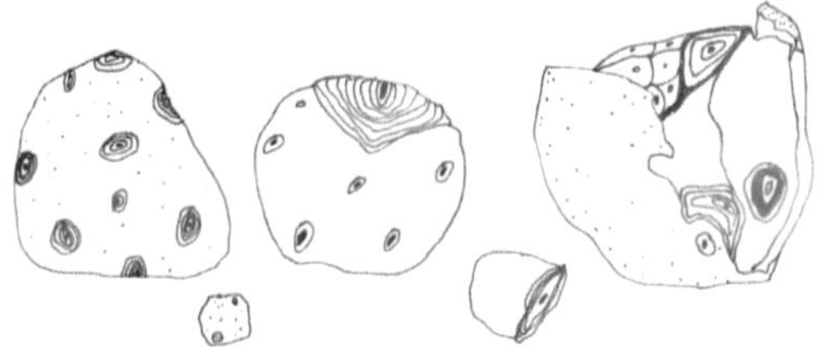

I woke up to the din of birds chattering and singing simply because they were alive and it was a new day. Faint light penetrated the gauze windows of our tent. Folding my arms under my head, I lay on my back, eyes still closed. I allowed my mind to drift into the unfolding day while the babble surrounding me reached a crescendo. The touch of a finger tracing circles on my forehead pulled me back to the present.

'Time to pack up and go home, *Mein Schatz,*' Anthon's voice crooned close to my ear, the circles on my forehead becoming larger, to encompass my cheeks, my neck. I cuddled closer to him, putting my ear on his chest to feel the reverberation of his voice.

'I know, I know; just two more minutes to allow me to surface completely,' I begged as I allowed my eyelids to unlatch. Hazy disks of coloured light wedged between my lashes.

'I'll start with the coffee so long,' he complied. 'It would be nice to be packed before the sun is up. We've got a long way ahead of us.'

This brought me back to reality. We'll be going home today, back to Windhoek. Tonight we'll be eating dinner on the stoep with our kids.

'Do you think we'll find more Omajowas along the way?' I asked while folding the duvet. I handed the bedding down to Anthon, already waiting at the foot of the ladder.

'I'll certainly keep my eyes open,' he replied. 'If so, Alexander will do his nut.'

'While Nic and Louise will be able to taste it for the first time in their lives.' It suddenly dawned on me they had never tasted Omajowa before.

I clambered down from the rooftop tent, now empty and ready to be stowed.

'Would you mind finding the Stanley for me?' Anthon instructed from where he was lighting a gas cooker to boil our kettle. 'I'd like to make us some coffee for the road.'

'Good idea,' I replied. 'I guessed as much last night, so I put it on the front seat. Will quickly rinse it for you.'

As we were pouring our coffee, a familiar voice called out to us.

'Got a spare cup for a friend?'

'Rob!' Anthon called out with a smile. 'Of course! Come and sit down for a minute.'

'There's something I forgot to tell you last night.' Rob perched himself on the chair he brought along the previous evening. 'I assume you'll be driving back over the Grootberg Pass today?'

'That's what we've planned,' Anthon confirmed.

'The road's been upgraded recently,' Rob replied, 'and there's a spot halfway up the pass, from this side, where you must stop.' He took a sip of coffee as he dug for his pipe in his trouser pocket.

'Why?' I asked, ever impatient. Perhaps it stems from not being a smoker. If no other benefit, smoking does seem to force the perpetrator to sit or stand still for a moment every now and again.

'Well, apart from the dramatic view, the contractors constructing the road created a bit of a borrow pit to the left of it. This opened some amazing stones. One can clearly see the agates in the broken pieces.' Rob smiled at me as he lit his pipe, knowing full well this news would get my attention. My hoarding habit appears to be legend. I've got a particular fondness for the rough blue agates one finds in Damaraland.

'Can you tell us a bit more about the geology of this area?' Anthon asked Rob. 'I know that it's one of the oldest parts of Namibia, geologically speaking.'

'The Etendeka Plain has a fascinating history,' Rob agreed. 'When the supercontinent of Gondwana still existed, it formed part of the massive Paraná-Etendeka area. This was the location of one of the fiercest volcanic eruptions in the history of our planet. It hastened the opening of the

South Atlantic Ocean and buried the region under two kilometres of lava of which roughly 860m are still in place.'

'Was that when South America and Africa parted ways?' I asked.

'It certainly contributed to the subsequent continental drift,' Rob answered.

'The astounding thing is one can still find exactly the same geological formations and rocks in the corresponding part of South America as one finds here.' Rob looked at us with his endearing half smile, pipe-head cradled in his hand, elbow resting on his folded leg.

'When did all of this take place?' I asked.

'Between 139 and 128 million years ago,' he answered. Like a proper knowledgeable tour guide should.

'Wow! That must be a shock to those people who believe the earth is only 6,000 years old,' I joked.

'Luckily they don't seem to choose Africa as a travel destination,' Rob returned my quip.

'How did the agates form?' I've been meaning to find out for some time.

'The short explanation?' Rob asked.

'As simple as possible.'

'These massive volcanic eruptions acted much like pots of caramel boiling over. Gas bubbles formed inside the molten lava. In time these hardened. Water full of salts and other chemical compounds seeped into the empty spaces and there you've got it; an instant wonderland of lovely crystals and other treasures.'

'Love it,' I smiled.

'Well, guys, you must be on your way and I must deliver my guests to the lodge,' Rob drained the last coffee from his mug, knocked the tobacco from his pipe and slipped it back into his pocket. 'Was great to have seen you.'

'Yes, we must get going.' Anthon got up from his chair.

'Lots of love to Elfriede,' I gave him a hug. 'We'll certainly stop to look at the rocks.'

After Rob left, taking his chair with him, we packed as fast as we could. I slipped the dirty cups and dishes from the previous evening into plastic bags and packed it in one of Henry's drawers. This time order and neatness wasn't the aim; everything would be unpacked and washed when we reached home anyway. Soon after, we were on our way.

'Don't we have to fill up here?' I asked Anthon as we passed the petrol station close to the lodge.

'Not Henry,' Anthon laughed, 'we'll easily make Windhoek. Remember, Henry has an extended diesel tank.'

As we reached the Palmwag veterinary checkpoint, there were two fully rigged rental vehicles standing in front of the gate, the drivers in a heated argument with the supervising policeman.

'I'm sure they're tourists not understanding that they're not allowed to take meat back over the red line,' Anthon said. 'I'll go and see if I can help them.'

I opened my window, not feeling like joining the row. Soon after Anthon came back, leaving the officer on duty with an armful of packaged meat. The tourists were shunted through the gate and it was our turn with the veterinary police. Our trip was nearly over so we had no more meat left. The cool box and the Engel were duly inspected and declared empty. We could also continue further.

'What was that all about?' I asked as we left the checkpoint behind.

'Same old story,' Anthon explained. 'Like us on a

previous trip, they couldn't understand why they must give up meat packed and bought at a butcher in Windhoek. Everything is vacuum-packed, still with the sticker of the shop where it was bought on it. It even says Windhoek on the label. Of course the buggers took everything. The tourists have two days of camping left, but no more meat.' Then he added, with a hint of sarcasm, 'and as we all know, shops, where one can buy provisions, abound in Damaraland.'

I merely shook my head. We'd been in a similar situation a while back. We also wasted our time arguing with the veterinary policemen.

'Weren't the policeman meant to burn the meat?' I asked.

'He promised them he would, but unfortunately he had to inform them he'd not yet had a chance to light the drum in which the meat is supposed to be destroyed,' Anthon answered, doing an excellent impersonation of the apologetic official. 'One can argue he didn't lie. They'll be starting the fire about now. In time for breakfast.' He laughed heartily.

If one chooses to live in Africa, one must accept rules are rigid as iron when they should be open to interpretation and infinitely malleable when they were meant to be cast in stone.

'At least I managed to persuade the guards to leave them their cheese and eggs,' Anthon added the postscript. 'They tried to con them into believing they're entitled to those as well.'

From here it was a short haul to the Grootberg Pass, which forms the geographical divide between the Etendeka Plateau and the higher altitude savannah surrounding Kamanjab.

'Wow, what an improvement!' Anthon exclaimed as we reached the resurfaced road hugging the side of the mountain. It meandered through a large herd of springbok grazing on the sunny eastern slope of the mountain. If it wasn't for their white underbellies, they would've melted into the hillside. They grazed on, uninterested in the passing of humans and their vehicles; a twitch of a tail or the momentary lifting of a head were the only signs they were real.

'They could be statues, planted here to impress the tourists,' Anthon quipped.

'Don't joke,' I replied. 'A colleague of mine was approached by a wealthy American client to design a lodge in the Caprivi. Part of the brief was a long entrance way to the reception area, flanked by a menagerie of true to life fibreglass animals. This in a region where a real elephant might walk into your front door at any moment.'

'Was it built?' Anthon asked, shaking his head in disbelief.

'No idea. My friend declined the project. The entire design had to revolve around *faux natural*; from artificial rocks, synthetic wood, ceramic granite, you name it.'

'Why would anyone want to build with fake materials when the real thing is available in such abundance?' Anthon wondered.

'Because they can, my dear. When money is no object, it's easier to tell materials what to do than to struggle against their inherent nature. Real wood needs to be maintained to keep its lustre, genuine granite might soak up fat stains and authentic rocks are heavy and expensive to cart around. Much easier to mould your rock *in situ* out of wire mesh, cover it with a layer of concrete and imitation finish and *voilá*, you've got a rock designed to specification.'

We rounded a bend. What appeared to my eye as a monolithic mountain unfolded into a series of cascading peaks. To our left, a small plateau opened up an endless vista over the Etendeka Plain. The level area next to the road was still littered with broken pieces of rock and scarred by the zipper tracks of a front-end loader.

'This must be the place,' Anthon agreed. He allowed Henry to roll to a standstill.

'And now for that flask of coffee you made us earlier; and perhaps a rusk or two? I'm sure there are a few left in the drawer.' My mouth started to water. We normally fill the Stanley with plunger coffee sweetened with a couple of tablespoons of condensed milk.

I pulled on a sweater to ward off the bite in the early morning breeze. Carrying the Stanley in one hand and two cups in the other, I scrambled onto Henry's bonnet, careful to seat myself on the sturdy chequer-plate edge. Anthon soon joined me with the last of the rusks. We dunked them into our cups to soak in the creamy coffee, before slurping them into our mouths.

'Did Emily bake these?' Anthon asked. 'They're really good.'

'Yep,' I replied, 'she still uses *Ouma* Let's recipe.' Emily is my right hand, my left hand and general maintainer of order in our house. She loves baking. I taught her to bake wholewheat rusks the way my mother used to. When the tin is nearly empty, she leaves me a note with the list of ingredients she needs for the next batch. A gentle reminder she's really the driver of the household.

'I now see the Etendeka in an entirely new light,' Anthon

swept his arm in a wide circle, encompassing the breathtaking panorama falling away meters in front of our dangling feet. 'It wouldn't surprise me one bit if a dinosaur had to walk by right in front of us.'

'Or a volcano erupted from one of those pointy pinnacles in the distance,' I added.

We finished our coffee. Anthon lit a cigarette while I took the opportunity to rummage around between the rocks. It was just as Rob had said: the stones which were cracked and broken by the construction machinery exposed a myriad of fascinating crystals. Some were speckled with tiny green stones while others revealed a fairy-sized cavern within, lined by glittering crystals. With my newly acquired knowledge, it was easy to see how the air bubbles, which formed in the molten lava, were filled by water, over time forming agates and crystals. I picked up a few blue-grey pebbles, the chipped or broken edges revealing the telltale layering so typical of the Namibian agates.

Back in Henry, we crawled up the remainder of the pass, enjoying the clarity of another perfect African morning. We reached the summit. I took a final look at the ancient expanse behind us before we continued our descent into the next, much younger, valley.

'Enjoy your last stretch of gravel, *Mein Schatz,* from Kamanjab we'll be back on tar. By the look of those clouds, we might be in for a thunderstorm later today.' Anthon pointed at the grey-blue haze rising in the south-east, out of which white cumulus heads were already starting to grow.

Around Kamanjab scattered *koppies* rise out of the grassland. White-stemmed *Sterculia Quinquelobas,* another type of Star Chestnut, soar from these piles of granite boulders, like sentinels of the Savannah.

As the landscape opened up in front of Henry and closed behind us again, I attempted to add all the new puzzle pieces of information into the bigger whole.

'You never explained to me how it happened that your German father, a born and bred Namibian, married an Afrikaans girl from South Africa's Eastern Cape region?' I asked, suddenly realising how many gaps still had to be filled to give coherency to the picture.

'They met as students at Stellenbosch.' In retrospect, I realised the answer was obvious.

'Of course!' I nodded, 'although, I do find it surprising your *Oma* and *Opa* didn't insist on sending your father to Germany to study. Did they not regard South African universities as inferior to those in Germany?'

'My grandfather wanted my father to study agriculture. He envisaged his only son taking over Eirup one day, and rightly wanted his education to be relevant to farming in Namibia. Stellenbosch University offered a degree in agriculture which was highly regarded in Germany.'

'So your mom and dad met as first-year students?'

'Not quite. My mother was a first-year student. She was also exceptionally pretty. My father, already a senior, drove one of only three Alpha Spiders in South Africa at the time.'

'Don't tell me, it was a convertible and bright red?' I interrupted with a giggle.

'What would you expect? My family never did anything in half measure. The fairy tale even included a grand German castle and a nasty old witch, in the guise of my *Oma*!' he laughed.

'So they fell in love, got married and lived happily ever after?' I needled.

'Well, they certainly fell in love. They got married not to

'bring shame on the family', to use the euphemism of their day.'

'Whaaat?' I burst out laughing. 'Your poor mom. I can just imagine having to break the news to her own Afrikaans family, never mind informing *Oma* Trude and *Opa* Richard.'

'Yep, it was high drama. When the wedding finally took place, my mother was already a bit more chubby than she deemed fashionable. To this day she refuses to look at any of her own wedding photographs. She went as far as destroying all the wedding pics in her possession.'

'It must've been a terrible shock to Trude to have a daughter-in-law who couldn't speak a word of German?' I asked. 'Did it take her long to get to her current level of fluency?'

'My grandmother had her ways and means,' he answered. 'Soon after the baby was born, she took her away from my mother until she, my mom, could speak fluent German.'

'You must be joking. Was that not a bit excessive?' I couldn't believe it possible.

'You can ask her yourself when you see her again,' he replied. 'As I already explained to you, there was nothing moderate about my *Oma*.'

'So she learned German in record time?' I had to ask.

'Within six months she was fluent,' he laughed.

'Have you got contact with your Afrikaans family?' I asked.

'Certainly. My dad was an only child, but my mom's brother also had four kids, roughly the same ages as us four. They're our only cousins. We spent our summer holidays with *Oupa* Andries and *Ouma* Bert in Jeffrey's Bay where they had a sprawling holiday house right on the beach. We used to do the family Christmas thing there. It was great fun. I still get on well with my cousins, although we don't see each other all that often.'

Henry gave a jolt as the gravel changed to tar. A few low buildings appeared on either side of the road. Anthon brought Henry to a halt at a crossing, but we continued straight to Outjo, leaving Kamanjab behind before I'd had time to register we'd entered the settlement.

The clouds were now towering high in the not so far distance. Directly across our line of travel, a mass of bulging white soared over a swirling base of vapour. Approaching it, a dark haze oozed earthwards from this mass, as if a celestial creature had opened a sluice to release its cumbersome burden to the forces of gravity. The sunny day faded into gloom. A plump raindrop crashed onto Henry's windscreen. Soon a torrent descended on the front window.

Anthon slowed the vehicle down to a crawl and switched on the headlights and the puny wipers, but the deluge was overwhelming.

A waterfall drummed on the roof, muffling the drone of Henry's engine.

Flashes of lightning streaked through the dusk.

Water covered the road and dammed up to its edges.

By now we could hardly see ten meters ahead of us. Two dim yellow spots appeared in the oncoming lane, grew slightly brighter and passed us like phantoms.

Beside us, the row of wooden telephone poles keeled over, one by one, in slow motion.

Abruptly the gloom lifted, the torrent on Henry's front window subsided into a drizzle and somewhere ahead we could discern a few beams of sunlight. Anthon and I looked at each other and shook our heads in wonder.

'It was absolutely awesome,' I grabbed the first cliche which came to mind, the one currently in vogue with our kids.

'What can one say,' he agreed, 'isn't this why I describe Namibia as bipolar?'

After the cloudburst we passed through fresh grass, already silver-tipped with seed, rippling at hip height. The sky returned to vivid blue. Innocent blobs of cloud drifted above, perhaps plotting to join forces in another onslaught on the savannah.

We drove through the village of Outjo. The signpost next to the road proclaimed it was 71km to Otjiwarongo. Without warning the vegetation reverted to scrub, the ground parched. Yet, looking around us, I could see at least three distant storm cells similar to the one we just passed through.

'Another reason why I never wanted to be a farmer in Namibia.'

'Meaning?' I asked, reaching for the Stanley. I needed coffee to chase the drowsiness away.

'It's an above average rain year. There are clouds and storms all around us; yet, for all I can see, this farm hadn't had a drop of rain this season. It's heartbreaking if it happens to be your farm. You're powerless to influence the weather. Next year it might be your turn while your neighbour suffers.'

I filled our communal cup while Anthon rolled down his window and lit a cigarette. 'It still stresses you, though,' I commented. We all joked about how Anthon would sit on the step leading up to our front porch every evening after dinner, with his cognac and a cigar, wondering when the rain would come.

'It does,' he conceded, 'even though it doesn't affect me that directly anymore.'

'Perhaps the cure lies in one of Marcus Aurelius' meditations,' I smiled, as I passed the coffee to him.

'What do you mean?' he asked, uncomprehending.

'Does a fig tree bear figs?' I replied, holding out my hand for the mug again, then perching it in the cupholder next to the gear lever.

'So I should ask myself, is Namibia a desert country? Does the rain fall erratically?' he answered his own question as he flashed me one of his wonderful smiles.

'I must say, *Mein Schatz*, a decent cup of Ethiopian from our Jura would be a welcome change to our Stanley-brew,' he added, draining the last drops from the mug.

'You never told me what happened to Eirup.'

My question was unexpected. I was entering not-so-happy-story territory.

At first he said nothing. Pensive, he finished the last of his cigarette.

'I was in my third year at medical school. We got two weeks' holiday for the entire year. I was tired. Homesick. I phoned home. Just a normal once-in-two-weeks missing-my-family type of call. My dad answered the phone. "So, what're you doing?" I asked. That rhetorical question one asks when you phone your parents on a Sunday afternoon. You don't really expect much more than 'sitting in the garden' or 'having coffee' or some other mundane activity.'

'"Packing" my dad answered. "Packing what?" I asked, oblivious to what was really happening. "The house. Everything. We've got to be off the farm in two months' time." His voice nonchalant, matter-of-fact. As if it was the sort of thing they did every weekend.'

'"What did you say?" I asked. I needed to hear it again. Deep down I'd hoped he'd tell me it was a joke.'

'"We're packing," he repeated.' This time his voice was low.

'I knew it was true. "Why?" I asked. "Why do you have to be off the farm?"'

"'We sold it," he answered. "We sold Eirup.'"

Anthon paused, did what he seldom does and lit another cigarette straight after finishing the first.

'I felt out of breath, as if I took a blow to my stomach. "I won't have holiday before that," I heard myself say, "I won't see Eirup again."' He inhaled deeply, allowing the smoke to slowly seep out of his mouth; to calm him down.

'So you never saw the farm again?' My heart ached for him.

'I had to make a plan. A close family friend, also a medical doctor, understood my predicament. He booked me off sick for a week. I drove back home and wandered around the farm. I tried to say goodbye to the only solidity I'd had in my life through all the years of being shunted between boarding schools.'

'But why? Why did your parents sell it? Why didn't they at least talk to you about it first?'

'My parents were spoilt rich kids, *Mein Schatz;* they lived in their own reality. My dad never wanted to farm. He wanted to be an academic. He received his BSc. Agrig with cum laude, which landed him an offer for further studies at Göttingen University in Germany. My mom refused to go. She wasn't prepared to live in a small flat which she would've had to clean herself, with a baby whose nappies she would've had to wash herself. And how could my father be selfish enough to even consider taking her still further away from her own family?'

For the first time, I detected a pinch of bitterness in his voice. Were the sins of the fathers visited upon the children, perhaps?

'Hans Hörlein chose well when he chose Richard Schröder as his heir. Farming was in *Opa* Richard's blood. He brought Hans Hörlein's dream to full fruition. The farm flourished. The Schröders of Eirup were prosperous and respected wherever they went.'

'At the height of their wealth, *Opa* Richard and *Oma* Trude retired to a luxurious villa in Spanish Farm, Somerset West.'

He took a couple of deep drags from his cigarette. I waited in silence for him to continue, in his own time.

'On the one hand, my parents were finally rid of the darkness and spite of Trude, on the other, they were never groomed to take over what was essentially a huge modern business. Two droughts hit the subcontinent during the next decade. Although my dad could still draw on his father for advice, he had to keep the business going. Profits dropped, but the number of mouths he had to feed on Eirup only grew. A good part of the surplus went to the old people, Richard and Trude, in Somerset West; my mother had a fetish for whatever money could buy. My sister told me, when they packed my mom's clothing, there were 27 dresses which still had their price tags on. Let's not even mention the shoes and the hoard of jewellery.'

He shook his head.

'Yet I was told to get a study loan if I insisted on studying medicine.'

He took another last draw, inhaling the smoke deeply,

then stubbed out the cigarette. 'But you asked why they sold it. My dad found that drinking enough alcohol made him forget. Then *Opa* Richard died. My father lost his tormentor, but also his mentor.'

'Hans Richard struggled on for another couple of years, drinking more and more. Some mornings he couldn't remember anything that happened the evening before. Eirup was still a coveted property and Richard Schröder was no longer around to prevent them from selling it, so my parents figured they could probably get enough for it to keep them going until well into old age. I can't tell you whether they discussed the matter with a financial planner or Trude or any of my siblings, but I certainly was never consulted.'

I took his hand.

We drove in silence for a while.

'Did you ever return to Eirup after it was sold?' I needed to know whether he reached closure. That's if one could ever reach closure after such a loss.

'A couple of years ago one of my uncles from Germany came to visit. He wanted to see the farm where his illustrious relative from Africa had lived, the one who helped them financially through the hardships of the Second World War.'

He must've registered my surprise.

'Yes,' he looked at me with a wry smile. '*Opa* Richard supported a number of family members through hard times. I've got another uncle who told me *Opa* Richard motivated him by promising to pay his schooling and tertiary education, on condition he'd improve his marks every year. He went on to become Professor Doctor Doctor. Yet *Opa* Richard's own grandson had to pay his own way through medical school.'

'You're referring to yourself, aren't you?' I said.

'Of course,' he answered. 'I only paid off my study-loan after I turned forty.'

Again a hint of bitterness?

'So my uncle came to visit and I phoned the then owner, Mr Z, the Afrikaans farmer who bought Eirup from my father,' he continued. 'A week later we drove out to the farm. Little had changed, except that Mr Z didn't have an inkling of Richard Schröder's refinement or breeding. He kitschified the grand old homestead with fake Greek columns and shiny ceramic floor tiles. But that was his business. What saddened me was the neglect of the family graveyard. It used to be my place of contemplation; the refuge where I went when I wanted to be by myself. I remembered the wind singing through the trees my great-grandfather planted. He and Marie were laid to rest there, eventually my grandfather as well.'

'My uncle wanted to see Richard's grave. At first I couldn't find the graveyard; then I realised the trees were all chopped down. The fence was rusted, the gate gone, the gravestones half covered with sand.'

'Back at the house, we were invited for tea. We sat in the garden under the huge trees, also planted by Hans Hörlein. Mr Z's grandchildren were playing on the lawn. When he joined us a bit later, I asked him why the trees in the cemetery were cut down. "I saw no point in watering them," he answered, "so they died. My neighbour told me it looked ugly, so I chopped them down." His air was insolent, his attitude and dress showed a lack of respect for these visitors of whom he knew little except that they were German.'

'I couldn't help comparing him with my grandfather,

ever the gentleman. Guests were always worthy of respect, whether German, Afrikaans or Damara.'

'Mr Z asked me whether I felt any nostalgia for times gone by. "When I played here as a kid, I never considered the possibility this farm might ever belong to anybody else," I answered. Then I added, "your grandchildren probably feel exactly the same way, but one day someone else's kids will be playing under these same trees."'

'"Never," he replied.'

'"Never is a long time, Mr Z." I held his gaze. "The only constant in life is change."'

Anthon took a deep breath, as if he'd just run a marathon.

'And? Does he still own the farm?' I asked.

'He sold it a couple of years later. His grandchildren are no longer playing under the trees,' Anthon replied.

I could swear I detected a whiff of satisfaction in his voice.

Chapter 19

IF ONLY I COULD GET INTO MY PATIENTS' HEADS

'We'll be in Otjiwarongo soon,' Anthon woke me from another semi-slumber session, which the coffee had failed to stave off. 'Let's make a pitstop under those trees. Once on the B1, it won't be so easy to pull off.'

He parked Henry under a large Camel Thorn next to the road. I welcomed the chance to stretch my legs and empty my bladder. I always carry a plastic shopping bag in the car, specifically for those pieces of tissue other women leave dangling on bushes or pushed halfway under rocks. They've got the mistaken belief tissue paper decomposes in no time. Believe me, it stays there for years, disfiguring some of our most pristine places. Urine is sterile, Anthon always tells me. Moreover, it's your own. Please just take it with you and dispose of it in a bin or a toilet.

'Perhaps it might be a good idea to switch my phone on.' Anthon fished for his mobile in the glove compartment. There was no cell phone reception west of Opuwo, and little in-between any of the towns.

'Still no reception. We'll have to wait until we get to Otjiwarongo. I need to phone Freda to find out what my day looks like tomorrow,' he grunted, not yet back in work mode. 'And I've got to clock in with JP. I don't unnecessarily want to trigger my Land Rover Recovery Plan.'

'And I need to let the girls know roughly when we'll be back home,' I added. As usual, when travelling like this, I lost track of time.

'When did we leave home?' Anthon asked me, a crafty smile on his lips.

'I don't know,' I answered absentmindedly, 'it feels like at least ten days ago?'

He gave a loud laugh. 'What day is it, *Mein Schatz*?' he asked.

'Well, we left Windhoek on Thursday morning,' I remembered, 'we spent the first night in Ruacana,' I counted on my fingers, 'then we camped one night at Hippo Pools, the next night we camped in the Skeleton Coast,' I had three fingers down, 'and last night we camped at Palmwag. That means today must be Monday? So we left home only five days ago?'

'Is it not amazing how travelling lengthens one's life?' Anthon replied, a smug grin on his face. 'But we've got to get going. It's still more than two hours to Windhoek.'

I clambered back into Henry with reluctance. I was looking forward to seeing the kids but loathed the last stretch of road to Windhoek.

We entered Otjiwarongo. Anthon's phone started to beep continuously as the messages came in.

'Back in civilisation again,' he grimaced.

'I'll read them to you,' I offered. 'The first one is from the mother-of-your-children. She needs money for ...'

'Skip it, please, I want to enjoy the last bit of our trip,' he sighed.

'So is the second and the third,' I added. 'Next, there's one from Freda, asking that you call her as soon as you can. Then one from your son.' This one was greeted by a visible intake of air.

'What does he say?' he asked. Communication with his boys was erratic.

'He needs money for a school outing,' I answered. 'The last one is from your mother. She needs medicine.'

'And I'm the Family Bank,' he groaned. 'Just switch off the damn phone,' he sounded exasperated.

'And Freda?' I asked. 'Shall I call her for you?'

'No. The signal will disappear once over that hill. Just message her and ask if there's anything urgent. I'll call her as soon as we get home.'

When we next had signal, the reply came in.

'Nothing urgent, but you're already fully booked for the next two days,' I informed him.

Another beep.

'Freda says Mrs M made an appointment. She wants to know whether she should allow an hour consultation again?' I relayed the message.

He nodded with a smile. I typed the reply and switched off the phone.

Anthon chuckled. 'If I could just get into my patients' heads.'

'What do you mean?' I asked.

'Take Mrs M for example,' he hesitated, considering how to explain his thoughts.

'She's sixty years old. The first time she came to see me, she believed she needed medication for her heart. I examined her thoroughly, but couldn't find anything wrong. I sensed something else was the matter.' He paused again.

'She was my last patient for the day. I asked her to sit down so we could talk about whatever was bothering her. I asked Freda to make each of us a cup up tea before leaving.'

'Over tea, Mrs M told me she couldn't sleep. She woke up at night in a cold sweat, worrying about her children. Soon this would worsen into heart palpitations and shortness of breath. "Why do you worry about your children so much? Surely they're old enough to look after themselves?" I asked her. She told me about her 32-year-old son; how he struggled to get the right job and earn enough money to buy a house which would satisfy his wife. And how her daughter had two young children who had to stay with the nanny while she went off to work. And how her daughter-in-law did *this* wrong and the son-in-law should do *that* etc etc etc. "Did the heart palpitations and the lack of sleep help your son to make his wife happy?" I asked her. "What do you mean, Doctor?" she asked, taken aback. "Well, lying awake all night and stressing your heart seems to be a strange way to solve your grown children's problems," I answered, shrugging my shoulders. "Let's put it this way, could your mother-in-law ever help your husband to make you happy?" I noticed the beginning of a smile dancing around her eyes. "Doctor," she answered without thinking, "my husband knew very well, if he wanted to make me happy, he needed to keep his mother as far away from me as possible." She burst out laughing. Then the irony dawned on her, "and I lie awake at night wondering how I can help my son to make his wife happy? Doctor, you're a genius." As she picked up her bag, I asked her, "so what medication exactly did you have in mind, Mrs M?" She looked at me with a roguish grin, shaking an extended index finger in my direction. "You know I don't need pills, Doctor," she replied. "You're extremely clever, do you know that?"

'So now, when she makes an appointment, you see her for an hour and she feels better?' I asked, amazed. 'Sounds like you should've become a psychiatrist.' I thought of all the different general practitioners I'd visited in my life. Except for one, a female GP, who became a good friend, most of them stuck religiously to the seven-minute rule. And I never left without medication or a prescription. 'Do you charge her for more than a normal consultation?' I had to ask.

'Why should I?' he answered, 'I enjoy talking to my patients. I'm always surprised at how many only need to voice their concerns to someone who's really listening to make them feel better.'

'But why do you say you want to get into their heads?' I

asked. 'You seem to be able to do it already?'

'With some patients it's easy. Take Mrs M, her husband is a busy executive and her children are living their own lives. At her age, friends are inclined to advise her to interfere in her children's lives, as that's what they all do themselves. Once I examined her and found nothing wrong, it was easy to find the problem elsewhere. With other patients it's not so *einfach*,' he used the German word meaning simple, which had become colloquial in Namibia, whether speaking Afrikaans, English, Damara or Oshiwambo.

'Give me an example,' I asked.

'I've got a patient who's been with me for ten years. She suffers from severe asthma and tends towards obesity.'

'The asthma shouldn't be a problem, though,' I interrupted. 'I thought allergology is one of your interests, your 'hobbies', as you often call it?'

'Except in her case the asthma only started after the age of five, and as yet we couldn't establish the cause. I can only treat it symptomatically, with medication. And her obesity is caused by obsessive eating. She's been to see a psychiatrist and regularly goes to a psychologist, but they don't seem to be able to get to the root of the problem.'

'Is it not unrealistic to want to cure every single patient?' I asked.

'Perhaps it is, but with some I just know intuitively there must be a way to better their quality of life. That's when I wish to get inside their heads.'

I looked at him, yet again wondering about his endless supply of empathy.

'You're an amazing human being, do you know that?' I said. He shot me a surprised look, as if considering the possibility that I was joking.

'It comes with the territory, I suppose?' he tried to laugh it off.

'I mean it,' I affirmed, taking his hand in mine and weaving my fingers through his. 'You're a special person.'

He lifted our intertwined hands and pressed my knuckles to his lips. 'Thanks for being my best friend in the world,' he said.

Henry hummed with satisfaction. The surrounding grassland waved green and silver. Two eagles floated like feathers in the cloud-dappled heavens.

'I suppose our chances of obtaining any more Omajowas are slim?' We were now getting close to Okahandja and the towering ant hills reminded me of our delicious meal at Hippo Pools.

'Fairly. I usually come across them on the other side of Otjiwarongo,' he replied. Then his face lit up. 'But we still have those two stems in the Engel.'

'You're right. Will you be able to cook them for us tonight? How many mouths can we feed with them?' The image of a family dinner started to take shape in my head.

'If we stop at the Portuguese on the corner, across from the mosque, we can pick up a couple of leeks and some cream,' he looked at me with expectation.

'We still have a piece of beef fillet in the freezer,' I started planning. 'It should feed us and four kids.'

He chuckled. 'Do you think it will be regarded as coercion if we lured the boys for dinner with fillet and Omajowa?'

'Possibly,' I laughed,' but it's still worth the try.'

'Done,' he agreed. 'Switch my phone back on and answer my son's message with "would you and your brother like to join us for Omajowa and fillet steak tonight?"

You can let the girls know we should be home by latest half past four.'

The Omajowa did the trick. The boys agreed to come to dinner. Anthon offered to pick them up from their mother's house. The girls would be dropped at five by their father. The last stretch to Windhoek was spent planning our evening meal and debating which wine would best compliment the exceptional flavour of the Omajowa cream sauce.

We passed through Okahandja in good spirits. Not even a packed minibus-taxi with a fully laden trailer, screaming past us around a blind bend, could dampen our mood.

I resented the narrow road between Okahandja and Windhoek due to the traffic congestion and the general recklessness with which many drivers travelled. That afternoon I concentrated on the green hills and woodland lining the B1.

My mind drifted to the house we'd moved into less than three months ago. We'd been renting separate townhouses since my divorce and Anthon's breakup. Good friends of ours lived in a dilapidated farmhouse on a large plot in the old part of Klein Windhoek. They were expats; Gerry an American and Tina a Dane. After a two year struggle with the Namibian Department of Home Affairs for residency permits, they just gave up and decided to move back to Colorado, where Gerry hailed from. They broke the news to us one evening as we were dining on their stoep. We were devastated, as they provided us with much-needed support during a difficult period.

'But we've got a bigger plan,' Tina had a roguish expression on her face. 'Why don't you consider taking over our lease? Together? There are enough rooms for the two of you and four children.'

Anthon and I looked at each other. To be able to move

into that old house, with its lovely ambience, would be heaven-sent. Not to mention sharing the rent and costs and being able to accommodate all the children, should the need arise. Anthon's divorce was far from resolved.

'When will you be leaving?' I asked, thinking it would take them at least six months to get their affairs in order for such a move.

'The removal company will fetch the container on 30 November,' Gerry answered.

'This year or next year?' September was nearly over.

'This year,' Tina laughed, 'in just over two months.'

Anthon looked at me. 'It's now the 25th. I need to give my landlord two month's notice.'

'Same here,' I agreed.

'So what are we waiting for? Let's get those letters out tomorrow.' Anthon gave me a high five, while Gerry and Tina fetched a bottle of champagne, shrewdly bought for this celebration.

And that was how it came about that we moved into the house on Von Eckenbrecher Street.

Hidden amongst enormous trees, it used to be a stable which belonged to the manor house of a farm, in those days on the edge of town. As Windhoek grew, the city swallowed the farm, which was subdivided into a residential area. The manor house and its stables were divided into two separate properties and the old stable rather haphazardly converted into a house. None of it was new or pristine, nor was it 'gentrified' or tarted up to conform to current fashion. It was simply an old structure, albeit with a charm of its own.

Crumbling in places, extended where the need arose, no two rooms had the same floor covering or the same floor level. Graceful old wooden doors and windows were interspersed with the most horrific standard steel frames. The roof was covered with the original, rather battered, corrugated zinc sheeting, which always leaked with the first rains of the season. Yet the house had one feature so delightful, one encounter was enough to make one fall in love with the place: an enormous verandah protected the entire front facade. This shady oasis became our primary living area; our *stoep*, as it is called in Afrikaans.

In summer we spent all our evenings on the *stoep*, around our quirky dining table. My artist sister-in-law welded a table base out of discarded fire hydrant pipes and full-bore outlets, transforming it into an intricate forest of steel kelp amongst which wide-eyed metal fish hovered. A single piece of rosewood, three meters long and as wide as the tree which gave birth to it, rested on this base. The wood was obtained from a colleague authorised to remove trees where power lines or roads had to be built, so I'd had no sleepless nights about the felling of this giant. A wing-backed sofa, which entered Namibia as part of Marie Hörlein's trousseau, had pride of place next to the front door, while our two Morris chairs, one inherited from my grandmother, the other from Anthon's Afrikaans grandfather, completed the seating arrangement. An old travel chest, also ex-Marie Hörlein, served as a coffee table and general hoarding surface.

We turned into Von Eckenbrecher Street. Anthon phoned Titus, who looked after the house in our absence. He came running to open the gate for us, a wide grin on his face. We drove underneath the huge Camel Thorn Tree, guarding our entrance, past the *rondawel*, or roundhouse, sublet to a yoga-instructress to help pay our rent. Then we entered our private back yard, green with lush wild grass.

Anthon brought Henry to a standstill next to the house. Maja, our Siamese cat, bounced towards us. Suddenly remembering we abandoned her for five days, she stopped in her tracks, sat down on the steps leading up to the *stoep* and nonchalantly proceeded to wash herself. We were strangers of no consequence. To make sure we understood just how deeply we'd offended her, she would ignore us for at least the next hour. Or until one of us dropped a few pellets of cat food into her food bowl.

Leaving Henry's engine to purr, Anthon patted him on the dashboard. 'Well done, once again, old chap,' he drawled with a British accent.

'And I thank you for always bringing us home safely,' I gave Anthon a deserving hug.

'Welcome back, Doctor!' Titus came towards us with a satisfied grin. 'Come and see how nice the house looks.' We'd completely forgotten Titus was going to use the time we were gone to repaint the exterior of the house. I rushed onto the verandah to see the result.

'What an improvement, Titus!' I complimented the work. The pale ochre we chose lit up the verandah. I could hardly wait to add our newly acquired rocks to the collection on the wide low walls demarcating the edge of our summer lounge. Titus looked on with satisfaction, deservedly proud of his handiwork.

At that moment the doorbell rang. 'The girls are back!' Anthon shouted as he pressed the button to open the gate. Soon Nic and Louise, heavily laden with rucksacks full of clothing, school bags, a guitar, bed pillows and a favourite teddy bear, staggered onto the stoep, dumping everything right there when they saw us.

'It looks as if you carted everything you own over to your dad's house,' I laughed, hugging them tightly.

'Alex and Luke are coming for dinner,' Anthon could barely contain his excitement, 'and we'll be having Omajowas!'

Louise started a 'Yipeee!' while Nic wanted to know: 'we'll be having WHAT?' Realising she also had no idea what an Omajowa was, Louise scrunched her mouth into an asymmetrical rosebud, her eyebrows pulled into question marks.

'The most amazing giant mushrooms I've ever tasted,' I explained.

'Unfortunately, we can only show you the stems, we already ate the tops,' Anthon barged in, 'but they were as big as THIS!' He made a circle with his arms, encompassing something larger than the circumference of an opened umbrella. Louise's eyes grew proportionately in size. 'I want to see them!' she shouted, pulling Anthon's arm while jumping up and down with all the gullibility of her eight years.

'Are you joking with us?' Nicola, five years older and much more suspicious, narrowed her eyes, suspecting a hoax.

I took the stems from the Engel. 'Well, make up your own minds. Perhaps Anthon might be exaggerating a tiny bit,' I laughed, 'but they were larger than the biggest dinner plate we've got in the house.'

'I just looove mushrooms!' Louise pirouetted around us.

'Come, I'll help you to get all your bags to your rooms before I go,' Titus suggested, happy the house was full of people again.

'And I'll make us the cup of coffee we dreamed about earlier,' Anthon offered.

Later that evening, as darkness seeped into the house, we lit the lamps hanging around the edge of the verandah. While Anthon fetched the boys, the girls decorated the table with brightly coloured table mats and candles. I prepped the Omajowa and made a large salad from greens picked up at the shop when we bought the cream and leeks; the fillet steak all ready marinating in olive oil and black pepper, ready to be grilled when Anthon returned.

Once the boys arrived, I was amazed at how easily the kids interacted when they weren't required to take sides in the games adults play.

'Dad!' Alex exclaimed after devouring his third slice of fillet, piled high with creamy Omajowa, 'you still make the best steak in the whole world.'

'Yes Dad, you do,' Luke agreed, slowly nodding his head in affirmation, his large brown eyes not letting the piece of fillet left on his place out of their sight.

On her way to the kitchen, Nicola slipped a disk into the CD player in the entrance hall. Soon Louis Armstrong's throaty voice proclaimed 'What a Wonderful World' it was. I felt Anthon's arms folding around me, his body gently swaying as he hummed his own version of the famous tune. We watched our kids, in animated conversation, enjoying the food, the sense of family. A pool of warm yellow candle-light bound us together around the table. For that moment, our past sorrows and the hardships still to come were outside this sphere of love and togetherness, skulking in the darkness where the flickering candlelight couldn't reach. Yes, everything is always exactly the way it should be.

ACKNOWLEDGMENTS

For always being ready to make changes to the cover, the graphics, anything related to the layout, as well as simply being there when I needed advice, I owe a huge thanks to my daughter Nicola Fouché, especially as she had to work long distance under difficult circumstances.

For the grammatical and structural edit, I thank Deepak Maharaj and Nora Kovats. Their contributions gave me clarity on so many grammatical and other issues encountered while writing this book.

For moral support and an unbiased opinion, I thank my daughter Louise Fouché.

For giving me the final push to publish and stop overworking my manuscript, as well as for being my most avid supporter, I thank Jasper Blome.

Lastly I have to thank my husband and travelling companion, Anthon Schröder, for providing me with a never ending narrative of wonderful stories, for always seeing the humour in any situation, for never getting tired of listening as I read and re-read the chapters out loud, and for being my best friend.

ABOUT THE ILLUSTRATOR

Nicola Fouché was born in South Africa in 1991. In 1998 her family moved to Namibia. Having grown up in a country bursting with far-stretching, highly contrasting landscapes and imagery, these places and spaces continuously serve as a basis for inspiration in her art practice. In 2015 she graduated from the University of Stellenbosch (South Africa) with a BA degree in Visual Art (Fine Art). From 2016 to 2020 she lived and worked in Shanghai, China. Currently she resides in Hermanus, South Africa.

For more about her work visit her website at www.nicolafouche.com

ABOUT THE AUTHOR

Lydia Schröder grew up in Stellenbosch, South Africa.

An architect by profession, she lived and practised in Namibia for eighteen years. With her doctor husband, Anthon, she travelled extensively throughout Namibia, both for work and leisure.

In 2016, when their youngest child left the house, they closed their practices, put their earthly belongings in storage and set themselves adrift on the business of life.

For the next couple of years they lived out of their suitcases, spending at least three months every year driving through the entire Namibia while Anthon did rural medicine along the way. Their wanderings took them from Germany to New Zealand, Singapore and Shanghai, while Anthon deepened his training and honed his skills as Ego State and Somatic Experiencing therapist.

When they needed a breather, they spent time in their wooden cabin overlooking the ocean in Hermanus, South Africa, where Lydia completed 'A yellow butterfly on an elephant's foot'.

In 2019 they stumbled upon a fairytale town in Bavaria, fell in love with a 15th century loft apartment overlooking the market place and decided to drop anchor for a while.

Please visit her website and blog at

www.lydiaschroderauthor.com

More information about Anthon's therapies can be viewed at

www.doctoranthonschroder.com

www.ingramcontent.com/pod-product-compliance
Ingram Content Group UK Ltd.
Pitfield, Milton Keynes, MK11 3LW, UK
UKHW041952190726
13854UKWH00005B/1923

9 783982 286426